GW00685083

THE
Spanish House

Publisher Beatrice Vincenzini & Francesco Venturi

Managing Editor David Shannon

Editor Tessa Fiume

Design Karen Watts

Translator Caroline Ball

Index Lynda Swindells

First published in the UK by Scriptum Editions

Created by Co & Bear Productions (UK) Ltd.

Copyright © 2006 Co & Bear Productions (UK) Ltd.

Text copyright © Co & Bear Productions (UK) Ltd.

Co & Bear Productions (UK) Ltd recognise Patricia Espinosa de los
Monteros & Joaquin F. de Santaella as authors of the work.

Photographs copyright © 2006 Francesco Venturi.

Printed and bound in Novara, Italy by DeaPrinting.

Colour separation by Bright Arts Graphics, Singapore.

First edition

10 9 8 7 6 5 4 3 2 1

ISBN 1-902-686-54-3

THE
Spanish House
ARCHITECTURE & INTERIORS

written by
PATRICIA ESPINOSA DE LOS MONTEROS ROSILLO &
JOAQUÍN FERNANDEZ DE SANTAELLA MARTIN-ARTAJO

photographed by
FRANCESCO VENTURI

SCRIPTUM EDITIONS

Antique Map of Spain & Portugal, 1808, by Thomas Bowen.

contents

Introduction

In Spain, as elsewhere, houses reflect an evolution of ways of life, customs and economic status, built to cope with the prevailing weather and to accommodate the requirements of everyday life and work. Several influences have determined the form of Spanish houses and, indeed, life. There is the unruly topography of mountains and valleys that criss-cross the peninsula; a climate that changes completely from one region to another as well as from one seasonal extreme to the next; the produce of the land itself, which can dictate a house's construction and needs; and then there is the human factor.

From the Iberians and Celts, through Phoenicians, Carthaginians and Romans to Visigoths and Moors, as well as independent pockets of culture such as the Basques, different peoples have left their mark here. The castle strongholds of the Castillian plateau and the noble *pazos* of northernmost Galicia, sturdy Basque *caserios* and sprawling whitewashed *fincas* of Andalucia, to say nothing of *masias*, *cortijos, haciendas, alquerias* ... all have their own specific regional characteristics and satisfying beauty that comes from eminent suitability of purpose.

The candidates for this book could have filled volumes - not for nothing does Spain have Europe's highest number of Unesco-designated World Heritage Sites. But we had to narrow our choice down - one of the most difficult tasks - to a selection that illustrated the multiplicity of features and idiosyncrasies contributed by Spain's very diverse regions. The houses we have chosen may not be the oldest nor most important, but their attraction is that they are owned by families who, whether they have lived in them for hundreds of years or only a few, love them dearly and in some cases have rescued them from ruin.

Spanish houses developed from two basic models: the Mediterranean *casa romana* and Celtic *casa celta*. The former, dominant in the south, were whitewashed, with a central courtyard, the *patio*, and a flat roof that doubled as a terrace. In the relatively benign climate, much of daily life was carried on in the open, focused on the *patio* and whatever other gardens the occupants could afford.

In rainier northern regions the *casa celta* was constructed in stone, with thick walls and a pitched roof of tile or slate. There would be fewer openings to the outside and these took the form of large covered doorways, and arches and galleries to give protection against cold and rain. The *zaguán*

acted as entrance hall, storage area and carriage and even animal shelter, and instead of an internal *patio* there would be a garden behind the house.

Inside, the houses of most rural working families ran along similar lines. Being largely self-sufficient meant that the house was both living space and agricultural store, with room to accommodate work and livestock. Many had stables and plough sheds, as well as carpentry workshops or forges, mills or presses ... and even, in some, a school.

The Iberian peninsula has been a battleground right from the earliest times, including nearly a thousand years of Reconquest against the Moors - the very word Castille relates to 'castle', a fundamental feature of the Spanish countryside. Even in rural areas, people tended to build houses in communities, for fear of brigands but also because of the poor infrastructure and communications in many areas until only about fifty years ago. Nobles' *casas señoriales* - never palaces - were always within a village or small town, while isolated towers served as defence and refuge, accommodating the local population during times of attack.

As peace began to bring political and economic stability, especially during Bourbon rule in the eighteenth century, many nobles followed the French or Italian fashion in enlarging and embellishing their houses.

In extending this vaunting of wealth to ostentatious exteriors, part of the very Spanish spirit of the house as a private reserve was lost.

Many houses suffered at the hands of the French during the Napoleonic Wars, but an even greater act of despoliation occurred during the middle of the same century. This was the *desamortización*, a long political process that came to a head during the reign of Isabel II under her minister, Mendizabal. Since the Church traditionally didn't pay taxes, its vast lands and possessions were financially unproductive, so they were confiscated by the Crown and sold in order to render them taxable and increase Crown revenue. This is why a considerable number of former convents and monasteries are now family-owned. From such changes in circumstance, layers of cultural complexity have been preserved, along with building methods that may be more ecologically and aesthetically acceptable than many of today's methods.

A more recent influence on the rural house is a twentieth-century phenomenon resulting from the Spanish approach to town versus country life. The 'country weekend' has led many town-dwellers to buy up modest country or village houses, impelled by a desire to escape the overwhelming consumerism and commerciality of urban life. Hundreds of village and rural houses have been given new leases of life in recent years, some by new owners, but also some by owners who had just kept them to

store unwanted paraphernalia. The future for this new type of exodus seems limitless - the time may come when the situation is even reversed, when second houses become first houses while a home in the city, increasingly difficult to live in, becomes simply a pied-á-terre. Food for thought...

Although interior design has been a secondary consideration, one of our aims has been to end the reputation that the Spanish pay too little attention to decorating their interiors. Some houses featured here contain works of art of great value, others not, but all of them, whether soberly restrained or colourfully high-flown, demonstrate a fine aesthetic sense at work, and the photographs focus not only on the impressive visual impact of some of these houses, but also the refined domestic detail.

We didn't intend to make this book an architectural treatise based on learned texts; there are historians and other experts enough for that. Rather, we aimed at a journey through Spain in words and pictures, lingering in places to appreciate the cultural diversity of the country, certainly, but also to explore the whys and wherefores of different house styles - and to describe the enchantment, the romance and mystery of a rare thing in this century of convenience and ease: of living in what was once a monastery, a castle, a mill or even a house that once bred silkworms.

Pazo de Rubianes

VILLAGARCÍA DE AROSA, GALICIA

Despite being the twenty-first century, this seems like a place where time has stopped. Here, the silence is broken by the ringing of church bells or the creaking of a bullock cart. This is Galicia, that most remote and mysterious of regions, full of superstitions, rituals and legends. On winter nights the moon fills the woods with her pallid gleam and around the warmth of a Galician *lareira* they tell tales of the Santa Compaña, the ghostly procession that foretells a death, of the Wolf Man and, especially, of the *meigas*, the local witches, because - as everyone agrees - 'they may be out there'.

Galicia, at Spain's north-westernmost tip, is traditionally seen as a poor region, rundown and cut off from the rest of the country. But it has had strong links to the rest of Europe since the early Middle Ages, via the cultural, philosophical and intellectual cross-currents that flowed and continue to flow along the Camino de Santiago. Pilgrims the world over would journey along this Pilgrims' Route that led almost to Finisterre, the end of the world, to pray before the tomb of St James the Apostle, and so news inevitably travelled to Galicia too, along with, at different times, the latest in fashion and science and construction techniques, in literature and medicine and medicinal plants. It is no coincidence that the first maize brought to Europe from America was raised at a *pazo* in Lugo, just to the east of Santiago de Compostela.

The large *pazos* that dot the Galician countryside among the mists of these far-off northern regions, have their origins in fortified towers, later becoming comfortable family residences surrounded by the land of their estate. They are often not far from towns and villages and nowadays many of them are caught in the fallout from an urban nucleus that has spread out and engulfed them. In more recent times *pazos* have regained their seigneurial status and put aside their medieval fortress image, even though at any given moment they could become judicial centres, with their lords charged with meting out justice.

The great bulk of the Pazo de Rubianes rises up like something in an adventure novel or a forgotten dream echoing down the centuries. It is said it was built in 1431 by Don José García de Caamaño, who founded Villagarcía and was first Señor of the House of Rubianes, a title that is one of the oldest in Spain and one of only three *señorios* that survive in the Spanish nobility.

Undoubtedly, he was one of the rebel nobles who confronted Pedro the Cruel, King of Castille, and built the pazo as a fortified house to defend himself against certain reprisal.

Of the original building there remains no trace; the archives note only the existence of a fortified tower and a chapel with a shrine dedicated to St Joseph. The *pazo's* present appearance is the result of a drawn-out series of modifications following a four-square plan in the eighteenth-century French fashion, with gargoyles and escutcheons decorating the cornice and façade.

The grounds have a history all their own, one that cannot be read in plans but in the thickness of the tree trunks, some of them world-champion trees. In the 13ha (32 acres) are to be found some of the most beautiful and oldest examples of Galician magnolias, their branches sweeping the ground; eucalyptuses with 14m (46ft) trunks; and rhododendrons, azaleas and camphor trees brought from India, to say nothing of trimmed box hedges and camellia walks that already, in December, are coming into flower. It is said around here that

renowned French landscape gardeners, called to Madrid to lay out the gardens of the Campo del Moro, later passed this way and left their indelible mark on the parkland and gardens of many *pazos*, including this one.

However, the French garden that now stretches out in front of the house is much more recent, made by the mother of the present Señor de Rubianes about 55 years ago. The main entrance was initially on another side of the house and the site of the present garden was a field enclosed by box hedges. Using French designs as her model, she traced out the pattern in rope with the help of her young daughters. There are parterres of trimmed

PREVIOUS PAGE *View of the* pazo *over the French garden, with its box hedges, maples and azaleas.*

ABOVE *One of the crosses that acted as a waymarker on the Camino de Santiago. They were always topped by an image of the Virgin Mary or a cross to wish pilgrims a safe journey.*

OPPOSITE *The pool known as the Frog Pond is ringed by stone columns; it is reached via a pleasant walk beneath plane trees and makes a good picnic spot.*

maples and azaleas in tones of fuchsia, red and purple, and in the centre is a seventeenth-century font, a gift from the parish of Villagarcía.

Pazos are usually two storeys high, with a low loft to help keep in the warmth. The typical layout is similar to other northern farmhouses: domestic rooms on the lower floor beside small pantries and the kitchen with its cooking pots over the open flames of the *lareira*, while on the main floor are the living rooms and main bedrooms. Sometimes there is a sun room or glazed gallery oriented to make the most of the winter sun.

The interior has a magically calm air, where time passes slowly. The Galician sun that appears timidly through the rain to shine on magnolias, azaleas and camellias also filters through the windows to illuminate the books in the library. Shelves full of legends concealed in endless files and archives guard secrets barely glimpsed in immortal scenes from novels of Galician life such as *Los Pazos de Ulloa*, or where Rosalía de Castro allows nostalgia for her native Galicia to come through in her writing, or texts that the political writer Jovellanos meditated upon in the gardens of Ribadulla.

According to the popular definition, a *pazo* is a 'dovecote, chapel and cypress'. The chapel is usually freestanding but attached to the perimeter wall, with two doors, one for the owners of the *pazo*, the other for the estate workers and those living nearby. In the courtyard there will also be the well, typically rather plain, and the *hórreo*. Seen all over the Galician countryside, *hórreos* are grain stores perhaps 20m (65ft) long, raised up on stone *rateiras* to put the harvest beyond the reach of rodents and the permanent damp of the Galician soil.

ABOVE *One of the paintings of Holofernes painted by the Duque de Rivas, great-great-grandfather to the present Señor de Rubianes, who was a painter as well as a poet. The bowl under the table is porcelain from Zuloaga.*

OPPOSITE *In the Salón del Arco, the marble busts of two Roman emperors face each other from their pedestals. The portrait on the wall is by Mosquera and there are also two paintings by Esquivel and one by Madrazo. The sofas are eighteenth century and the rug is Persian. The wooden fire surround has been restored.*

BELOW *In the main living room the walls are lined with red and strawberry-coloured damask. Notable here are a seventeenth-century painting of an archangel and a magnificent Carlos III mirror. The marquetry table dates from Carlos IV (late eighteenth century) and the clock on it is of Imperial white marble. The rug is, again, from the Real Fábrica and the chandelier is English crystal.*

ABOVE *The staircase carpet came from the Real Fábrica, the royal carpet and tapestry factory. Among the portraits hanging on the walls are Queen Isabel II as a child and one of an ancestor.*

OPPOSITE *The dining room walls are lined with red Egyptian cotton, with walnut panelling to dado level and again at ceiling height. The paintings include two by Margarita Cassi and two by Arellano. On the mantelpiece is a silvered punchbowl and a pigeon-shooting trophy won by the owner's grandfather.*

ABOVE AND OPPOSITE *The library is one of the most important rooms in the house. The bookcases, which reach almost floor to ceiling, are made of chestnut and house some 2000 volumes on the themes of religion, heraldry and French history. On the walls are framed letters, testaments and odd documents such as the one that names the founder of this house as inquisitor of Galicia and mayor of Villagarcia. A portrait of the previous Señora de Rubianes (above right), painted by her sister, hangs in a corner of the library that serves as an office and around it are displayed plans of the garden and family crests.*

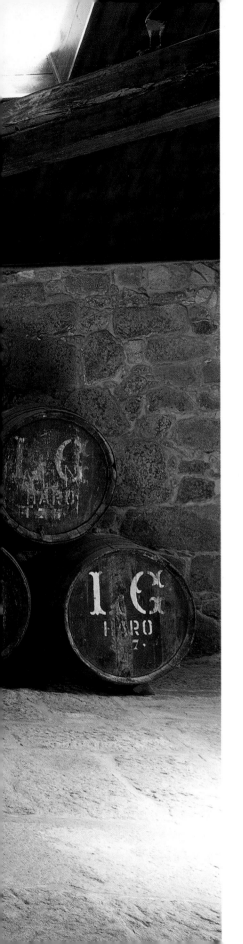

OPPOSITE & ABOVE: *The wine-making room, still with its ancient wooden grape press. The walls and floors are stone embedded with oyster shell, used locally instead of cement. In the same room is the old* lareira *for cooking (above), with its bread oven.*

OPPOSITE *The house dates from 1431, but was destroyed in the seventeenth century and had to be rebuilt. The chapel, dedicated to St Joseph, dates from 1538 but is still the original. The magnolias around the house are more than 200 years old and are recorded as being among the best in Galicia.*

ABOVE *The trunk of a eucalyptus that measures 14m (46ft) around – another nearby has a circumference of 10m (33ft). They are believed, along with trees at Oca and Santa Cruz, to be the oldest in Galicia.*

RIGHT *The hórreo for storing grain. This is a modern one but no house in Galicia is without one.*

Caserío de Otalora

BELTRÁN DE HORMAECEA, PAIS VASCO

As the plane descends to Fuenterrabía on a clear day, the scene spread out below is typical Basque farmland, *caserios* in miniature dotting the green hillsides and escarpments, each with its own well-manicured field of maize, vegetable garden and straw loft.

A *caserio* might be described as the truly Basque farmhouse. The Basque country - País Vasco - straddles the westernmost part of the Pyrenees, with one foot in France and the other in Spain, separated by the mountains and the River Bidasoa but united by a language and customs, maintained down the centuries, whose origins remain very uncertain.

Caserios are found from Castro Urdiales on the Bay of Biscay across the border to Les Landes and the form they take depends on when they were built but also the wealth of the region or of the owners - the oldest ones are to be found in El Goierri and the richest in El Duranguesado. Some have façades plastered in a style called *a matallana*; others have their beamwork painted blue or red, and all are roofed in old tiles. They may or may not have a glazed-in *galeria* but the gateways and entrances always carry mysterious signs and symbols - signs such as a strange cross etched into a window frame or the *lau-buru* symbol, signifying the beginning and the end. And you will see *eguzki-lore*, a flower that grows in the mountains, hanging from the oak lintel of a door to ward off the witches who, at the time of the full moon, are said to emerge from their caves up on the peaks of Amboto, Mugarra or Zugarramurdi.

Traditionally, a house would convey other messages too. A check on the windows, for example, would say whether the household included young girls of marriageable age - a new coat of whitewash signalled that a daughter was ready to wed. This meant she had finished weaving the 200 *varas* of linen needed to make her trousseau, linen that would, to cap it all, have been woven from flax grown on the family's land since she was eleven years old.

This strict tradition, which regulated family life in a *caserio* until well into the twentieth century, finally fallen by the wayside, but other ancient ways are still adhered to. Family life here is martriarchal, and in *La Casa Española* the historian Ginés Sanchez Hevia recounts how the real head of the family group is the mother; it is she who organizes life in the house, manages the family

finances and sells the produce of the kitchen garden at market. The husband just looks after the animals, splits wood and tends the crops.

According to tradition, there are also rules dictating how a *caserio* should be built. Construction would begin with an 'ash stone' to mark the kitchen hearth. From this central point a circle 494m (1620ft) across would be traced, marking the limits of a rectangular, almost square, house in the style of the *casa celta*, with no inner courtyard.

Things are no longer so, but a *caserio*'s layout follows the old model, which is the most logical for a house where the family lives under the same roof as their animals. Many *caserios* were, in fact, two homes under one roof, side by side or back to back, to accommodate the households of more than one generation. Generally, the house has two storeys, plus a large loft under the roof to provide storage for grain and straw. The main entrance is usually in the east-facing wall but protected by a deep arch, big enough to provided a sheltered area where open-air work such as winnowing, wood-cutting or cleaning chestnuts goes on.

Inside, the focus of the ground floor is the

kitchen, with *txitxilus*, benches with fold-down backs, around the hearth. Around the perimeter of the kitchen will be necessities such as the bread oven, the press for the local chacolí wine or stores for farm equipment.

On the upper floor are the family rooms,

DETAILS: *A stylized cross (left) etched in to the window frame as a good luck sign, the stonework round a window (centre) brought into relief by the* matallana-*style plasterwork and an* eguzki-lore *over a door (right) - this relation of the thistle features in legends about warding off witches.*

with broad chestnut floorboards and whitewashed walls. Furniture might be austere and cumbersome, but made of sound wood - stout oak chairs with rough-shaped legs, tables of chestnut and, in the bedrooms, high beds with painted headboards and enormous wardrobes with mirrored doors. There would be large wooden storage chests, too, adorned with hunting scenes, flowers and fruit or with geometric patterns symbolizing the universe and reminiscent of Celtic funerary designs.

In this region the name of a house is often an indication of its owner - Lopetegui means

Lope's house; Pedrorena, Pedro's house - or the owner's chosen profession: Sastrebaita is the house of the tailor. The name Otalora links this house to the name of a clerk to the first king of Durango who, like many powerful men of the time, owned land and built *caserios* to house his farmhands.

In the eighteenth century Durango was a power in Spain thanks to its ironworks, timber industry and mills, and the wealth that these brought with them also brought about a transformation in the region's *caserios*. Façades were made grander, archways were added, and dressed stone gave them the look of mansions rather than labourers' houses.

Although Otalora has the date 1750 carved on the façade, this refers to the year it was renovated and enlarged; the house was originally built in the second half of the sixteenth century. We know this earlier date, not from archives or records, but because the construction methods of *caserios* have been studied in such detail that they can be dated to within fifty years.

The *Caserios* present owners acquired the house only quite recently. The state they found it in was lamentable, but, under the supervision of the owner, work is now coming to an end. Each wall and stone has been salvaged, many layers of limewash and old floor coverings have patiently been removed until the original seventeenth-century features emerged: oak beams in the walls, chestnut floorboards and ceilings, stone window-frames and doorways, as well as many individual features such as the miller's steps, restored to help conserve the original spirit of the house. The interior has been furnished, little by little, with pieces found in local markets or antiques shops to complete the final effect.

With centuries of tradition resting on the Basque *caserios*, they now have the opportunity for a second life, as many of them will become country hotels or, like Otalora, second homes for city folk.

ABOVE *A pine dresser containing a collection of English and Spanish china and pottery soup tureens.*
OPPOSITE *The dining room is situated in part of the former stables, and has internal windows because this wall was originally the outside wall of the house until the stables were added in the nineteenth century.*

LEFT *The so-called 'miller's steps' are typically found in caseríos and have been made in the same way since the sixteenth century. They are solidly and simply constructed in oak, with no handrail or risers, but the individual treads slotted into the staircase's sides.*

BELOW *Exposed wall beams are a common feature in caserios. The beams served to strengthen the walls and were a more economical form of construction – although all-brick walls were not unknown they were expensive and chiselled stone was usually preferred.*

OPPOSITE *Beside an old leather wing armchair in the sitting room is one of the original window openings that has been kept intact. The internal walls of caseriós were painted to help keep the house clean and dust-free, and traditional colours were red, white or indigo. The owners found many of the walls painted this rich red, and maintained the tradition.*

OPPOSITE & ABOVE *Various rooms go off the upper landing. The floorboards and beams here are new, as originally this was the open space of the straw loft, but the high ceiling meant that there was room to fit in bedrooms and bathrooms. The church pew (above) is seventeenth century and made of walnut, and the cabinet (above right), also seventeenth century, is Aragonese, decorated in the* arte povera *style.*

RIGHT *A guest bedroom, situated above the dining room, is furnished with simple, low beds in scrubbed wood known as* camas de aña. *The big curved beam that spans the whole space is found in every Basque* caserío.

OPPOSITE *The original staircase, which has had some sections extended. This gives a good view of the wooden framework of the building, and the pleasing play between vertical and horizontal beams. This distinctive forms of this construction method has been studied in great detail.*

OPPOSITE *The characteristic entrance porch to the* caserío, *with its flagstone floor and skirting, was open-sided but provided shelter against inclement weather so that some of the farm's tasks could be carried out under it. The seat was originally a church pew.*

THIS PAGE: *The stone arches of the two house that once made up this* caseríos *meet at this column (above), which would often be engraved with the date of construction. Typically, the plaster would leave exposed the stonework framing windows and doors (above right). The armrest-cum-table of the* txitxilu *(right), a traditional kitchen benchseat, which would also serve as chicken coop and where, near Christmas, even turkeys would be housed.*

Casa de los Begoña

VILLA DE SALVATIERRA, PAIS VASCO

Salvatierra, in the province of Álava, is in the heart of the Basque country, not far from Navarre. Approaching from Guipúzcoa to the north-east, the mountains flatten out into a burnished valley, the Llanada, which is a reminder that the dry interior of high Castille is not far away.

Villa de Salvatierra's streets are studded with casas *señoriales* with family crests on their façades. This is an important way of 'reading' the history of a Basque house, especially in Salvatierra where in a single street there are probably a dozen houses carrying coats of arms, nearly all belonging to the same family. Facing the church is what is obviously the largest: a tower house with a rear garden and a façade emblazoned with the inevitable coat of arms. Once the Casa de Ordoñana but now the Casa de los Begoña, it has been in the same family for almost five hundred years, but passed through the female line, which is why it has been known under a number of names.

Inheritance by the eldest child was the norm in the region, established to avoid the dispersal or division of estates – the eldest male child received everything and the younger siblings had a right to nothing (a system similar to the Catalan *hereu*). But with inheritance came obligations: he had to look after the rest of the family, ensuring they lacked for nothing, providing a roof over their heads if they had nowhere to live, arranging his sisters' marriages and providing their dowries. (Traditionally, while the eldest son inherited, the second son went into the military to serve king and country and the third went into the Church.)

Casa de los Begoña was built when Villa de Salvatierra was reconstructed after a fire in 1564. A feature of the stone frontage is the corner balcony, which probably harks back to a Castillan style by then defunct elsewhere. But why a Castillian-style house here in the Basque country? Because at times in its fluid history, the town belonged to Castille. Historically, this is a crossroads, witnessing the coming and going of one ruler after another and passing between monarchs and nobles like small change.

Alfonso El Sabio, the Wise, had granted the town semi-autonomy by a *fuero* or charter in 1256, and changed its name from Agurain to Salvatierra de Álava. In 1371 it was incorporated fully into Castille, but just a few years later, it was invaded and fell under the rule of the kingdom of

Navarre. After a number of battles and pacts, Salvatierra was returned to Castille, and Enrique II promised it would never pass out of the Crown's hands. But the king failed to keep his word and in 1382 he ceded the town and seigneurial lands to Don Pedro López de Ayala, chronicler to the last three reigns, whom he made Conde de Salvatierra. This secession lasted 140 years, until 1520, when the count was among those who rebelled against Carlos V (who was also Holy Roman Emperor) during the Revolt of the *Comuneros*. The brave hero who vanquished the count and earned the favour of the emperor was none other the count's nephew, Martín de Oquérruri. Pedro López de Ayala, Conde of Salvatierra, was condemned to death and died in prison in 1524, and his descendants never again owned Salvatierra or its estates.

Many years later, Martín de Oquérruri's grandson had this house built, to provide - as was normal among the landed gentry - roots

PREVIOUS PAGE *The main façade, as seen from the street, with its escutcheons and corner balcony.*
OPPOSITE *View of the garden and the rear façade, which shows more clearly the remains of the battlements of what was a fortified tower-house before being partly demolished by the king's troops.*

and stability for the family. Since then it has been passed down through the generations, its history reflecting the loves and wars associated with the town.

The principal façade, which faces on to the Calle Mayor, is of dressed stone, but the house was originally built for defence, and this is more obvious in the remnants of fortifications that can be seen on the rear. It was probably at one time a tower that was partly demolished by an overlord as punishment for some act of rebellion, and was later converted into a house.

The interior has undergone numerous changes, such as the glazed *galeria*, which is an early nineteenth-century addition, and the garden, where there survive two yew trees that are about 300 years old. The most recent modifications were by the grandmother of the current owner, who came into possession of the house in the early twentieth century. Ana de Ardanaz had been married to Manuel de Begoña and lived in Bilbao with her four children, but she was widowed very young and took over the houses and lands she inherited in Álava and Rioja as the only niece of the last owner. Her arrival in Salvatierra caused excitement in the town and among her own family, who hardly knew her - she was a young widow, very rich, and she came to be known as

La Niña de Oro, the golden girl. It was she who introduced numerous modernizations in the house, changing its layout and making it much as it remains today.

Among pieces that catch the eye in the house are a number of carved wood desks and several religious paintings, notably an Ascension by Mariano Salvador Maella. In the drawing room is a precious spinet and a magnificent collection of books, including works by Francisco de Quevedo and a fine collection of incunabula. The books' subjects say more about the history of the house than many archives. They cover religion, the law, heraldry and Basque coats of arms; there's a good collection on the history of papacy, several volumes of Quixote, a collection covering the French Revolution, works by Fray Luis de León and St Teresa – in fact, a library that has evolved to reflect interests down the ages, from religious themes to liberalism.

'It's an incredibly traditionalist house, one through which the history of Spain has passed,' says the present owner. 'During the six years of French domination in the War of Independence, French troops devastated our house, as they did many others. Later, in 1837, during the Carlist Wars, the house supported Carlos and would give overnight shelter to generals and aspiring leaders such as Zumalacárregui, although the liberals also occupied the place... Among many souvenirs, we have here the swords, berets and military trappings of Lizarraga, the Carlist general who lost the final battle in the final war, the Battle of Estella, against Primo de Rivera. Rivera received the title Marques de Estella while Lizarraga, my ancestor - a romantic faithful to his ideals to the end - accompanied King Carlos VII into exile, dying in Rome a ruined man. As a legacy he left almost nothing except his swords, decorations, gold uniform buttons and his red beret... A thousand memories, grown up over so many years, nearly 500 years. Yes, a thousand memories. If the stones could speak...'

OPPOSITE *The small oratory is on the upper floor. Its altarpiece features the Virgin of the Pillar, along with statues of St Joseph and of the Sacred Heart, to whom the house is dedicated. On the altar and the walls are framed papal bulls and blessings.*

ABOVE *A corner of the dining room, with its oak panelling, on which are displayed a collection of Russian coffee pots and bronze pestles and mortars.*

RIGHT *A close-up of the Spanish desk seen opposite. It is considered exceptional because it is complete – the lower section of these pieces rarely survives intact. On it are displayed a collection of lacquered silver pill-boxes and other small boxes, along with family portraits.*

OPPOSITE *Looking from the drawing room through to the library. On either side of the doorway stand carved wooden desks, a Dutch one on the left and a Spanish one on the right. The flooring is oak boards and the beams have been left exposed in the whitewashed ceiling.*

OPPOSITE *At the beginning of the last century the grandmother of the present owner made major changes to the house and the dining room was refashioned. The walls are part-panelled in oak and the corner chimney has an overmantel of tiled panels of family coats of arms. The leather chairs and oak table are both Spanish. The table is laid for a meal with a Basque cloth and Bidasoa china.*

ABOVE *The galería was added to the upper floor in the nineteenth century and its windows look out over the garden. It is one of the most-used rooms in the house since it is sheltered and sunny in winter.*

LEFT *A marriage chest containing part of the trousseau. The child holding a rabbit in the portrait above it was a great-uncle of the present owner.*

RIGHT *The winter dining room on the upper floor has actually been converted from a small sitting room.*

LEFT AND OPPOSITE *The library holds a fine collection of Quixotes and several incunabula, as well as volumes on heraldry, the history of the papacy and the French Revolution; there are also works by Fray Luis de León and St Teresa. The seating here is Spanish and hanging on the bookcases are family crests belonging to the house.*

LEFT AND ABOVE *The stone entrance way has enormous doors that lead to the former coach house and the garden. The Ascension on the wall is by Maella. An antique iron lantern hangs from the ceiling and on the Spanish table are various copper dishes.*

RIGHT *Beside the stairs leading up to the house is a Basque trunk with, above it, a stone escutcheon belonging to a former family house that has been sold.*

Casa Popular

PEDRAZA, CASTILLA Y LEÓN

It was in the fifties that Madrid-based interior designer Paco Muñoz heard about a small town in the province of Segovia called Pedraza. Unsure of what to expect, he jumped on his Vespa with his wife and went off to see it. He says he still remembers that first sight of the town bathed in the sunlight of an August afternoon. There was nothing resembling an inn to stay in, so they lodged that night in a private home; and by the next day he was half-owner, with his brother Antonio, of a house in the town. Years later he bought the nearby house in which he currently lives.

Like so many places in Spain, Pedraza is full of history, which can be read in every corner and on every façade. Hispania provided the Roman empire with more than one emperor, and many historians consider Pedraza the birthplace of Trajan, the emperor who incorporated Dacia (present-day Romania) into the empire.

Paco Muñoz bought his first house in Pedraza from Cayetano Cabanyes, a noted Madrid architect. 'I paid just 14 thousand pesetas for it, but we are talking about 1955, remember,' he says, 'and there no phone, no running water. Pedraza was a ghost town. My plan was to do up that house to encourage friends who might be interested in buying others, and at least we would restore them carefully, no aluminium window frames, for instance.'

The town took notice of what he was doing, and in due course the mayor, Don Mariano (who died only recently aged over a hundred) remarked to him one day that all the young people were leaving for Madrid, to the extent that there were only two children in the local school. Could he think of anything that might help? It was then that Paco Muñoz decided to set up a metal workshop for the boys and a furniture and crafts workshop for the girls. These are still up and running.

'They were good times in Pedraza, surrounded by friends but few tourists,' the designer goes on, 'but bit by bit that changed. There is an aerial photo,' he adds, 'in which you can see just one single vehicle in the town, whereas now there are at least five hundred.' Nevertheless, the peace is still absolute in his library, which is where Paco spends most of his time when he is in Pedraza, peaceful despite the fact that its balcony is above the front door which, of course, opens on to the town's central *plaza*.

It is here in the library that Paco takes out a sheet of paper and draws, still wonderfully well despite being over eighty 'and without my hand shaking' as he remarks, while he explains the layout of the house. What he bought back in the fifties was, in fact, two houses that had been made into one. The doorway of one dates from the eighteenth century, and on the garden façade of the other (which at one time served as the locals' club) is the date 1808 - the year Napoleon looked as if he had securely conquered Spain, and also when the two houses were connected. 'A bit of a labyrinth,' says Paco, 'but it works from both sides.'

The first house provides the dining room and his wife Sabine's workroom, while the second, where the living room is, was the old cow byres, complete with manger. 'Here there are two levels, and in times gone by the cows would come down the stone steps into the stableyard and out into what is now the garden but was then a field. All that remains from the original field are two enormous box trees that are said to be over six hundred years old.' Later, Paco and his family bought two other adjacent small houses, which is where the library is now housed and through which one can pass into the *invernadero*, conservatory, and the garden.

There is also the modern extension, which houses the art collection they call 'the museum'. From time to time they take out different pieces and put them on display around the house. 'It's good,' says Paco, 'to have somewhere in the house to appreciate these pieces of art together, because if one or other is always to the fore, there comes a time when you no longer see it. This is why the Japanese don't hang their paintings, but keep them rolled.' Works of art in the collection also include pieces by Jorge de Oteiza and Eduardo Chillida, the sculptor who had also been a great friend since they were at architectural school together.

Memories and stories about the house and the area abound, as they must do after so many years. In particular, Paco's brother Antonio remembers the time that Grace Kelly, already

PREVIOUS PAGE *A small herb garden with, at its centre, a limestone fountain that began life in the sixteenth century as a baptismal font. In the background is the rear of the two houses that were made into one in 1808, according to the inscription that can be read on the façade.*

OPPOSITE *The stone stairs that link the two levels in the living room. On the wooden pedestal at the top is 'Homage to Kenso Tange' (1964), a sculpture by Jorge de Oteiza.*

Princess Grace of Monaco, passed a siesta asleep in one of their rooms. Another great memory is of when Antonio played bullfighter.

As is customary in towns and villages throughout Spain, streets leading into the Plaza Mayor would sometimes be blocked off to create an enclosed space where bulls would be released for a *corrida*. Bullfighters and picadors would leap into the improvised ring, watched and cheered by an impassioned crowd. Since he has always been an aficionado of all the arts, Antonio one day leapt into the *plaza* to finish off the fight with a bull. This earned him 'two ears and the tail', which in bullfighting terms has come to mean a outstanding performance awarded by those parts from the animal which the matador has fought and killed.

And speaking of improvisations, there should never be forgotten the golf course that a group of friends established in a nearby juniper thicket, at a time when this was a sport seldom played in inland Spain, and is rather

unexpected even today in the neighbourhood of a town over 1000m (3300ft) above sea level and considered utterly 'lost' among the uplands of Castille.

As Don Mariano the mayor recognized, Pedraza, like many Spanish towns, suffered a phase of depopulation from the migration of so much of its populace to Madrid. In fact, according to the 1900 census, the town had more than 900 inhabitants, but the most recent recorded only 450. But this is showing signs of rising as incomers have discovered the advantages of distancing themselves permanently or sporadically from the big city. As Paco comments: 'It's always better living out in the country or in a small town. I chose the small town because I think the balance of life and the ambience is a good one. You still have life and people around, especially here, where many houses have been bought by friends who have begun to appreciate the advantages of getting out of Madrid for the weekends.'

OPPOSITE *A corner of the* invernadero *that has been added to the house. Its aluminium and glass structure is protected by sun-blinds, and in winter it is one of the nicest and most used rooms in the house. A collection of antique birdcages and glass vases are kept here.*

LEFT *Another view of the lower part of the sitting room. In the old days, the stalls for the cattle were here.*

BELOW *The dining room is situated in the former granary. It has very a low ceiling but large French windows give direct access to the veranda and the garden.*

OPPOSITE *The two levels of the sitting room provide two defined living areas. This is the lower area, which is at garden level, and a wrought iron balustrade runs around the upper level.*

OPPOSITE *A view of the library that shows the two levels. In the lower part is a linen-upholstered armchair and low table covered with a linen cloth on which are displayed a collection of forceps, baskets and a birdcage. The painting on the back wall is by Francisco Farreras.*

ABOVE *Joining the two houses together created a large double-height extension, which has become the library. It is divided into a working and reading area in the upper gallery and a living area below, which is on the same level as the sitting room and the garden.*

RIGHT *This display table in one corner holds books and a variety of collectables.*

LEFT *The wooden staircase leading from the invernadero, conservatory, to the upper level of the library.*

OPPOSITE & RIGHT *One corner of the conservatory's working area is devoted to drying flowers. In the foreground is a chest of drawers and tools and baskets are stored on the shelves. The work table (right), laden with twigs, seeds and other necessities for the dried-flower arrangements.*

OPPOSITE *The guest bedroom. The beds, which date from the end of the nineteenth century, have bronze baldachinos and* toile de Jouy *drapes. At their feet stand a pair of Fernando VII chairs.*

ABOVE & RIGHT *A polychrome cope chest (above), on which are displayed objects as varied as locks, carvings and ceramic figures. The artwork on the wall is by José Maria Labra. The staircase (right) leads up to the main bedrooms.*

THESE PAGES *Being so sheltered, the* porche *(opposite &*
below) is used almost all year. It provides a summer dining
area that opens up directly from the indoor dining room.
The sofas are wicker and the table made of glass and
bamboo. It is a cool corner, protected by a climber-clad
pergola. The stone columns of the pergola support pine
cross-beams (left). A view of part of the garden with
cypress trees and a path edged in box.

Can Perramon

VENTALLÓ, CATALUNYA

Arriving here is a bit like trying to reach the Capitol in Rome in 390BC: any stranger's approach is alerted by a flock of geese. They go cackling by, looking at the newcomer furtively and then, when least expected, utter a range of alarming squawks that could wake the stones of the place, leaving the visitor paralysed to the spot.

Not that this is Ancient Italy, although Ampurdán could be taken for Tuscany, and nor is this a Roman house, although there are similarities. This is Can Perramon, one of the oldest *masias* of the Ampurdán region. Its origins go back to the twelfth century, when it was fortified like a castle and surrounded by lands that stretched to the horizon, although what surrounds it nowadays is the town of Ventalló, which has grown up in its shadow. The history its walls tell is one of complex lineage involving the peasant farmers and their lords who shaped these lands, and is a reflection of the history of Catalunya.

A *masia* is the typical farmhouse found in Catalunya, as well as down to the Levante around Valencia and in the Balearic Islands. Like a Roman villa, it would be the principal house on a piece of land, usually the home of the landowners and their workers, and perfectly adapted to their requirements. The design and layout varies, depending on the crops and animals raised on the farm, but all *masias* have a number of features in common that differentiate them from other rural houses. They would customarily be built on high land, to signal the land's ownership clearly, have two storeys and a solid appearance, with masonry walls and a pitched roof of Moorish tiles. Floors would be either of wooden boards or oiled terracotta flagstones, while the inside walls were traditionally coloured with earth-based pigments and oxides mixed with lime. On the lower floor an entrance hall led to the living quarters of the farmhands, to the stables and the kitchens, while above were the owners' bedrooms and the *golfas* or lofts in which to store grain. One unvarying condition that makes a house a *masia* is its *mas* or farmland. So, strictly speaking, Can Perramon is no longer a *masia*, since the lands once attached to it were sold off to those who farmed them.

All that remains of the medieval castle that one stood here are a few walls in the town square. When the Perramons were ennobled in the seventeenth century and married into the Caramany

family, they pulled down the castle and used the stone to build the house and also Ventalló's church. They called themselves Ciudadanos Honorables de Barcelona, a first hierarchy of gentry (equating to the Castillian *hidalguia*), indicating their wealth and pretensions to nobility. In 1664 (a date that can be seen carved into several doorways), the house was divided into two. The rooms behind the main façade were kept as accommodation for labourers, maintaining the rustic character of a *masia*, but the part that opens on to the *plaza* was converted into a more sophisticated *casa señorial*, with French furniture, paintings and decorative details that gave it a quite different character, faithfully following the styles of the time.

Can Perramon belongs to a descendant of the Fontcuberta family that, though a complicated mix of political marriages and the local inheritance laws of *pubilla* and *hereu*, includes the Caramany, Armengol, Recasens and Ferramon families. For centuries they held these wealthy lands that once included six municipalities, but with the passage of time they fell into decay and in the 1940s were sold.

But there remained one last romantic wedded to the history of his family and to the land that had belonged to his ancestors, who decided to buy the *masia* and set the house in order: Carlos Aguilera y Fontcuberta, Conde de Fuenrubia.

By the twentieth century his grandfather, a very rich gentleman with many estates and many children, was living in Barcelona and found he was visiting Ventalló only once a year. So he used the contents of the house, and four others, to fill an enormous one he had built in

PREVIOUS PAGE *The half-round archway entrance of the main façade.*

ABOVE & OPPOSITE *The* zaguán, *with its stone floor, stone framed windows (above), and wooden beams that hold up the house. This is where the farm's carts were brought under cover and the livestock kept in individual pens. The owner found the painting that now hangs on the far wall in the attic, damaged and discarded. It was by an unknown painter called Traggia whom he later discovered was buried in a chapel in Barcelona. He restored the portrait and brought it here. On the other wall is the Fuenrubia coat of arms.*

Vich. By the time Can Perramon came into the hands of Carlos Aguilera in 1962 the house was in a sad state of repair, and he has been quietly restoring it ever since.

The living room has been created from the long, narrow granary - a feature of all *masias* - on the walls of which are depicted the six municipalities that were once part of the family's fiefdom. Here and throughout the house are a diverse collection of pieces that have caught the eye of Carlos Aguilera, who during the 1970s had one of the leading antiques shops and galleries in Barcelona.

From the living room you cross a beautiful Italianate arcaded gallery into the garden. Once a kitchen garden, it is now encircled by a screen of cypresses and columns that half-hide a swimming pool, green-lined to give it the appearance of a natural pool.

The kitchen has also had a great deal of work done to it. Its lofty ceiling has been restored, as has the enormous hood above the *llar del foc* or hearth. As in every *masia*, this is traditionally one of the most important rooms in the house, where all life went on: cooking, washing clothes in the sink with ash, and where the farmhands would warm themselves from the ledge around the fire. Another typical feature were the *festejadors*, benches set beside the kitchen windows, where courting couples and newlyweds (the *festejadors*) could distance themselves a little from the rest of the family.

A formal garden, somewhere to stroll, was not a feature of the old *masias*, but there would always be the orchard as a welcoming approach to the house. One detail never missing (although many have since disappeared) was the sundial on the main façade, acting as an indicator of the owner's financial well-being.

There is a tradition, still referred to in stories today and similar to one in the Basque country, which says that, before building a house, an owner should plough a furrow to mark out the perimeter of the house, lifting the plough-share to denote where the future entrance would be. Not to follow this tradition would be to call down some disaster in the construction. These are old legends...

OPPOSITE *In the spacious inner hallway of the* casa señorial *part of the house everything is original - floor, arches, vaulting, alcoves, doors - except the busts of Roman emperors on pedestals, which were added to lend the room a somewhat Italian look.*

OPPOSITE *Access to the house is via stone steps without a handrail. The doors are very rustic-looking since this was the part of the masía where the farmhands lived. The faded red colouring comes from lime and earth pigments.*

LEFT AND BELOW *A passageway at the end of the zaguán opens out into a tiny courtyard with a well and decrepit stone steps that lead up to the house and on which is carved the date 1666.*

BELOW *The stairs that lead out of the kitchen to the inner hallway which gives access to the dining room. The clock and the brass pots and pans are antiques, and the wood-fired stove has been preserved from the room's original layout.*

ABOVE *The kitchen walls are painted in terracotta- and sand-coloured checks all the way up to the ceiling, which in this part of the house are up to 6m (20ft) high. The corner fireplace is original and the enormous hood was reconstructed and finished off with a stone column.*

OPPOSITE *This room beside the dining room was formerly the farmworkers' kitchen. The chimney breast is in the form of the rounded roof tiles favoured locally. The floor is covered with matting and the table and matching benches are Andorran. The wall recesses are used to display a collection of Spanish white ceramics.*

ABOVE *The eighteenth-century-style main bedroom still has its original vaulted ceiling. A separate sleeping area, behind curtains hanging from a foliated arch, contains a bed from Olot, near Girona. Paintings hanging here include* The Four Seasons *by the eighteenth-century painter Crusells.*

OPPOSITE *In the main dining room are upholstered Louis XIV chairs and a folding table. The brass chandelier is Dutch and the paintings are by, the reknowned Spanish artist. Miguel Rasero.*

ABOVE *In one corner of the galería is the outline of an ancient spiral staircase that leads up to the top of a tower and the dovecote.*

OPPOSITE *The galería, which is linked via steps to the living room and to the garden and pool. The arches date back to the eighteenth century, and although it is now filled with plants, this was where grain was once spread out to dry.*

BELOW *At the end of the galería is an old cistern that collects rainwater from the roofs and feeds it into the garden's irrigation system. The owner designed the garden in a very Mediterranean style, a mix of Italian and Moorish with rows of cypresses and hidden statues.*

Palacio de los Chaves Mendoza

TRUJILLO, EXTREMADURA

Night is falling in Trujillo, and going to dine with Don Duarte Pinto Coelho means climbing almost to the top of the old city, crossing streets and alleyways and squares large and small barely lit by street-lamps, to reach the *aljibe*, the Roman cistern that stored water in the upper part of the town. Then a sharp twist to the left leads into a square overlooked by the doors and balconies of the Palacio de los Chaves Mendoza. The door opens and we are ushered through the hall and across the inner *patio* to what must be the best terrace in the world. A cane awning keeps off the night dew and from the terrace is the reward of an incomparable panorama of the town and surrounding meadowland - whoever said the sky is blue had never contemplated an Extremeñan dusk.

It is here, in the heart of Extremadura, in this cradle of navigators and adventurers, in this town full of once-forgotten palaces, that Don Duarte Pinto Coelho has made his home. He is one of the liveliest and most cosmopolitan characters one could ever wish to encounter. Portuguese by birth, he moved to Madrid in the 1950s just when things (and especially houses) began to change. Pinto Coelho was one of Spain's first interior designers when such a profession was practically unknown, but what he considers himself to be is, above all, a compulsive collector; he himself describes it as more of an illness than a pastime. He takes advantage of travelling for work or to visit friends to learn more and buy more. And whether he is in Camden Town or a market in Jaipur, at eighty he is still up with the latest trends in decoration. He maintains his own, highly ornate style, traditional but with certain flashes of humour, which makes his house so individual, so full of history and of stories.

'I wasn't the first to come to Trujillo; a group of us came together - friends, including the Whitneys, a wealthy American family. They bought this house at the time that Fleur Cowles bought hers and the Mayans and Salases theirs. In those days we would come down to Pascualete, the *finca* that the Condes de Romanones had close by, to spend the summer. Back then, Trujillo was a forgotten town; nobody knew anything about it. We came and rediscovered it and, full of enthusiasm, we formed the Friends of Trujillo Association. We restored the town, gave it back the importance it merits. Today people still buy houses here, although the prices have sky-rocketed.

'But it was Mary Lou Vanderbilt Whitney who discovered this house and became captivated by it even though it wasn't for sale. It was part of an old foundation belonging to some nuns who ran it as a rest home for the elderly from Hurdas, a rocky, remote region in northern Extremadura. They weren't planning to sell it, but thanks to Carmen and Javier de Salas negotiating with the bishopric the nuns were persuaded to sell it in return for a well-equipped new home on the outskirts. Then we commenced upon a very careful restoration and soon there was heating installed, floors and doors renovated and they had bought all the furnishings they needed.

'Meanwhile, I was doing up a small house in the countryside nearby, and so seven years passed. The Whitneys would come to Trujillo to spend the summer with their children, and other friends followed, renovating more houses in the town. Just when everything seemed satisfactorily settled into a routine, Mary Lou presented herself at my door one day to tell me they had decided to sell the palace and, of course, to sell it to me. They realized it would be much more convenient to move into my house on their Trujillo estate and they wouldn't have to organize everything from so far away. She suggested a good price, so I bought it from her and found myself with two houses. I then sold my other one, which left me with just this house - a white elephant to maintain, but a marvel in its own way. It has its own special charm and atmosphere and the wonderful garden, which I've enlarged bit by bit and which has almost cost me more than the rest of the house, but I am so proud of it. I've made what the French call a *jardin de curé*, helped by Olga Mayans, a great friend and a great gardener.'

Although in the town the house is known rather pompously as the Palacio de los Chaves Mendoza, in its owner's judgement there is little of a palace about it. It was originally a monastery of the barefoot order of San Pedro de Alcántara, and its chapel and *patio*, the two

PREVIOUS PAGE *View of the house over the orange tree courtyard and, in the distance, the belltower and cupola of the chapel.*

OPPOSITE *The entrance hall. Flanking the doorway leading through to the* patio *are two eighteenth-century Spanish figures representing angels carrying lanterns. Above the door is a wooden bas relief of the Holy Spirit. On the left hangs some English crewel work embroidery and on the right a seventeenth-century painting above a Spanish table with a nineteenth-century Talavera earthenware bowl on it.*

most important parts of the building, date from the end of the seventeenth century. The chapel was originally larger and included the main entrance, through a doorway in a side-arch by which the monks would enter, but as part of his renovation works, Pinto Coelho changed the entrance to a more logical place.

The main staircase is his own design, inspired by a staircase in the Camerino de la Virgen at the monastery of Guadalupe, to replace one whose size was out of keeping with the house.

On the lower floor, ranged around the inner *patio*, are the living rooms, dining room, kitchens and various points of access to the gardens: the pool garden, the kitchen garden, the rose garden and the orange tree courtyard.

The upper floor includes fourteen bedrooms; five of them, all along one corridor, were former monastic cells and are christened Cornelia, Hobbs, Henry, Heather and Marionne after the Whitney children. The rest open off

OPPOSITE *This room has direct access to the garden and the collection of straw hats from various sources adorning its walls has given it the name of Salón de los Sombreros, Room of the Hats. The ceramic donkey on the table is eighteenth century, from Alcora.*

the upper gallery and each has a decorative theme built around a different collection: one with painted glassware, another with votaries and reliquaries worked by nuns, another with watercolours of interiors and yet another of nineteenth-century needleworks of dogs, while Don Duarte's room has Neapolitan gouaches as a theme. 'There so much everywhere,' says the designer, 'years of buying, collecting, enough to drive you crazy. It's an ailment like any other – if I buy one thing I have to buy twenty; that's my downfall.'

Here is a man who knows almost everything about the Spanish and their houses. He knows that an urban Spaniard used never contemplate living in the countryside or even visit it for weekends, and so houses in villages and country towns became cold, abandoned, inconvenient places which, like a tailor's chest, accumulated all the things that nobody wanted in town. But he has instilled in many Spanish friends a desire go out to the country, to live nearer nature, to appreciate its big old houses or, as in his case, to acquire old houses in abandoned towns and give them a new life. Of this, he can justifiably be proud.

OPPOSITE *The patio, with a lemon tree and other plants in pots. All the main rooms in the house open on to this inner courtyard – the living rooms, study, dining rooms, kitchens and games rooms on the ground floor, and the bedrooms above.*

BELOW *One of the stone-arched galleries running round the patio that have proved the perfect place for the designer's many and varied collections. Notable here are the pieces of Spanish rustic furniture and the ceramic panels displayed on the walls.*

ABOVE *Displayed on the chest are two eighteenth-century marble busts and a seventeenth-century processional cross with, on the wall behind, a collection of Hispano-Moorish tile panels.*

OPPOSITE *The music room on the upper floor, which is more used in winter, includes two grand pianos. The chimneypiece was designed by Don Duarte to incorporate a marble bas relief of Fernando VII and holds pieces of eighteenth-century blue and white china. The portraits of four Spanish monarchs include Isabel I alongside Carlos V, Felipe II and Felipe III. The sofas are upholstered in Genoan velvet.*

RIGHT *This tapestry of escutcheons and heraldic emblems is seventeenth-century French and the two portraits are of kings of Saxony. On the table (eighteenth-century Spanish) is a blue and white Talavera water jug and a collection of lacquered Russian boxes.*

OPPOSITE *A living room/study next to the terrace. The furniture here is largely Spanish, although the wardrobe on the far wall, which serves as a bar, is Dutch. Pieces here include an important collection of Chinese boxes with straw marquetry and a small part of the designer's large collection of eighteenth- and nineteenth-century Neapolitan gouaches.*

BELOW *A seventeenth-century three-seated choir stall, which came from a cathedral. The upholstery is red velvet and the gilded headrests incorporate cardinals' crests.*

ABOVE *Don Duarte had this staircase built following the design of one in the nearby Monastery of Guadalupe. The portraits on the walls are English from the seventeenth and eighteenth centuries.*

OPPOSITE On the walls of the large dining room hangs a series of four large paintings of Roman emperors from the Zurbarán school. The chairs are Spanish 'Queen Anne' and the yellow and blue rug is a very rare Ziegler Persian. The lanterns hanging from the ceiling are eighteenth-century Spanish and the table is laid with silver and pewter candlesticks and flowers from the garden.

ABOVE The plastered shelves above the fireplace are used to exhibit a range of ceramics. Hanging either side of the fireplace are two engravings by the Italian neoclassical engraver Giovanni Battista Piranesi.

RIGHT A small informal dining room containing plates from Puente de Arzobispo and seventeenth-century still-lifes by Josefa Ovidos. The ceramic figurines on the table are Portuguese.

ABOVE *One large chest displays nineteenth-century Talavera ceramics with, hanging above it, an antique heraldic panel.*

OPPOSITE *The corridor, which runs round all four sides of the patio at first-floor level, is furnished with chests and portraits of Roman emperors, and carpeted with Persian and Portuguese rugs.*

BELOW *One of the twelve portraits of Roman emperors that are found all around the bedroom corridor. This one hangs above a Spanish table and a collection of reliquaries in the shape of arms.*

OPPOSITE *The chapel. Its floor, copied from a church in Toro, is a chequerboard effect formed of granite and slate. The pews are antique pine with hand-forged nails and the pulpit is draped in embroideries and hangings.*

ABOVE & LEFT *The high altar with, on either side, antique embroidered panels. A hidden staircase behind the altar leads to a tiny camerino or dressing room in which are kept the various adornments belonging to the Virgin Mary's statue in her altar niche. A precious eighteenth-century carving of St Michael the Archangel (left) stands in its own niche.*

OPPOSITE *The swimming pool is set close to the house walls in a secluded spot, very sheltered and hidden from neighbours' eyes. There are trained lemon trees around the pool and a roofed area for relaxing and changing.*

RIGHT *Much of daily life is spent on the terrace in all seasons, as the cane awning overhead keeps out the cold and the heat. It is furnished with painted bamboo furniture, a great many plants and an odd collection of pottery.*

LEFT *On the terrace beside the orange tree courtyard a seventeenth-century Sevillan fountain provides the sound of running water, a Moorish influence that is an essential element in every Spanish garden.*

Castillo de Galiana

TOLEDO, CASTILLA-LA MANCHA

A July afternoon, and in Toledo the heat feels like the breath of a thousand demons. But the journey is worth it. Behind the station a lane leads up to the Finca de Galiana and a few minutes after passing the guard on the gate (interrupting his lunch of almond gazpacho), there comes into view the full majesty of this Moorish stronghold overlooking the Tagus. Overlaying its multifoil arches and Mudejar brickwork is a certain Renaissance influence, from when Carlos I (known to the wider world as the Holy Roman Emperor Charles V) made Toledo capital of the first empire on which it could be said the sun never set.

The Castillo de Galiana is steeped not only in history but in legends. One tells of how Galiana, the graceful, beautiful daughter of the town's Moorish ruler Galafre, fell in love with the son of the Frankish king Pépin the Short and embraced Christianity so that she could marry him. He, in time, was crowned as the emperor Charlemagne: *Galiana of Toledo/ her beauty a marvel/ the most celebrated Moor/ in all Moorish lands.*

Romance, legend and fact mix freely in the history of the castle, which served as palace to various kings of Castille. Alfonso VI is said to have lodged here when laying siege to Moorish Toledo in 1085, and no doubt added to its military air. But the greatest changes to the castle occurred in the fourteenth century when Alfonso XI gave it to his lover, Doña Leonor de Guzmán, who completely reorganized the rooms along the north façade. The life of this noble woman came to a sad end when, after Alfonso's death, King Pedro the Cruel ordered her death by that very Spanish form of capital punishment: the garrotte.

Some five hundred years later, the castle passed to Eugenia de Montijo of Granada who, through her marriage to Napoleon III, became the Empress Eugénie. Her major restoration work was still going on when she died at the age of 94. Galiana was inherited by one of the empress's descendants, who in 1959 sold it to Alejandro Fernández de Araoz and Carmen Marañón, who in their turn immediately undertook the third great restoration of the building. The castle's archives record that 'the building appears divided in two parts, that which constitutes the castle proper, and the Alberca, that was found completely filled with earth at the beginning of the most recent

restoration in 1959.' The castle today includes two towers and five vaults, the remains of Christian paintings and fourteenth-century inscriptions reminiscent of Granada's Alhambra. It was Carmen Marañón who brought the garden back to life, adding to the castle's history of strong female influence. Without them, it could be said, its famous Huerto del Rey, the King's Garden, would have been inconceivable.

In the Middle Ages the gardens here were said to be among the most beautiful in the world, enhanced by the proximity of the river Tagus. Moorish historians wrote of clepsydras or water-clocks and a series of great wheels that watered the orchards while swallows swooped among the arcades, and a sixteenth-century traveller wrote of *norias*, water wheels, scooping water from the river to irrigate 'that place full of trees and fruit'. To stroll under a summer moon among the myrtles, the air scented with night-scented jasmine and lavender, is a delight. The poet José García Nieto has more recently written: *One day/ who knows how/ I knew your name/ but on moonlit nights/ I called you Galiana.*

According to Alejandro Fernández de Araoz Jr, the name could come from the biggest cattle drovers' road from Portugal to France that ,officially, passes through the castle's land – called the 'Galias' drove.

PREVIOUS PAGE & THESE PAGES *The castle's restored façade, with the cobbled patio and part of the gardens, with avenues of lance-shaped cypresses and climbing scented jasmine. The gardens once contained pools, fountains, a water wheel and even a pavilion with a glass cupola over which water cascaded.*

BELOW *From the vaulted Galería de Galiana there are views over the Tagus and the old kitchen gardens. The castle's entrance is through the door in the caliphal archway at the far end.*

ABOVE *The* galería, *with its columns and lobed arches, looks out of the castle's* patio, *which hangs like a balcony above the river Tagus. The capitals of the columns carry the Guzmán crest.*

OPPOSITE *At the top of the tower, reached by a spiral staircase, are benches and, resting on the terracotta floor, old* tinajas *that once held oil or wine. In the mid twentieth century Doña Carmen Marañón de Fernández de Araoz undertook a major restoration of the castle and its gardens with the architect Don Fernando Chueca Goitia.*

Cigarral de Menores

TOLEDO, CASTILLA-LA MANCHA

Essayist, biographer, endocrinologist, historian and a highly enquiring mind on all subjects, the Madrid physician Don Gregorio Marañón Posadillo (1887-1960) was probably Spain's best example of a twentieth-century humanitarian. It was his finely tuned sensitivity that led him, in the 1920s, to acquire this house. *Cigarrales* are a symbol of the city of Toledo and this is one of the few that survive of the twenty-two that the Golden Age dramatist Tirso de Molina wrote about 400 years ago.

Dr Marañón invested an inheritance from his father in the restoration of this great monument, which was then bombed and ransacked during the Spanish Civil War. The doctor himself went into exile during the war, but on his return and thanks to the strenuous work of his daughter Carmen, he was once again able to enjoy his *cigarral*. Half a century after his death it is owned by his great-grandson and namesake, the architect Gregorio Marañón Medina.

The Cigarral de Menores was built in the seventeenth century for a monkish order, explains Don Gregorio, and it remained in religious hands until it was confiscated by the Crown in the infamous politico-economical *desamortización* of the mid-nineteenth century. It was founded in 1612 by Jerónimo de Miranda, a priest at Toledo Cathedral, for the Italian Order of the Minor Clergy. 'It's ironic,' he adds, 'that my grandfather should have lived in a house called "de Menores" - of the Minors - when throughout his career he had a special interest in the elderly and is known in Spain as a principal founder of gerentology as a medical specialism.'

He goes on to say that the word *cigarral* has a curious provenance: 'According to English visitors, the word comes from "cigar", while others trace it back to the Arabic term *figueral*. However, I'm sure that anyone who has spent a summer's day here will know that the deafening chirruping of cicadas (*cigarras*) is without a doubt the source of the name.'

Whatever the etymological origins, *cigarrales* are quite individual properties, specific to Toledo. They might be described as semi-urban, semi-agricultural, looking down on the city from the encircling hills. They are generally of simple construction with brick walls and a stone roof.

The Cigarral de Menores, built on two floors to take advantage of the slope of the hill, is roofed with Moorish tiles and stands among a series of terraced gardens full of almond and apricot trees, figs and the ever-present olives. The garden is criss-crossed with mysterious paths that lead to unexpected places such as an ancient well or, a little further on, the latest and sobering archaeological discovery was made here: a sixteenth-century bathroom exactly on the spot of, or rather below, the swimming pool.

Inside the house an important original room to be preserved is the chapel on the ground floor, which was badly pillaged during the Civil War. In it is a beautiful painting, the work of the nineteenth-century *costumbrista* artist Valeriano Bécquer, who was inspired by the *cigarral*'s former state of ruin. The chapel has direct access to a covered entrance beneath three arches. From here, a staircase decorated with an important collection of *cuerda seca* glazed tiles leads to the upper floor and what were, in its days as a religious house, the monks' cells. These have been converted into bedrooms with windows that open on to a view of the city.

It is well known that the best place from which to admire Toledo is undoubtedly the Camino de los Cigarrales. The city can be seen from the terraces of any of the *cigarrales* along the route, the cleft cut by the river at its foot and the soaring spires of the Gothic cathedral at its pinnacle. It is a scene that changes colour with the time of day: 'Bone grey in the morning, almost invisible in the blinding midday light and rosy in the evening like a blushing cheek,' as Pérez de Ayala described it in one of his books.

Books are an essential element of this house, which has its own library full of photos and rare volumes. To prevent this collection of so many dedicated, annotated, illustrated pages becoming the grazing territory of mice, it is protected by a sensor that emits an ultrasonic sound described as 'the squeal of the aggressive male rodent'.

Illustrious visitors have left their benevolent spirits in the library and rooms of the *cigarral*. Marie Curie has been here, as have Alexander Fleming, the philosopher Miguel de Unamuno and Benito Pérez Galdós although perhaps one of the best-remembered occasions was the recital that Federico García Lorca gave from his renowned *Blood Wedding* in the Plazoleta del Cigarral. 'That was what life here was like

PREVIOUS PAGE & OPPOSITE *The cigarral's north and east sides. There are a number of stone columns and fountains (previous page) placed in strategic locations around the cigarral. This column (opposite), erected on a brick base, has been topped by an iron weathervane. In the background is a narrow staircase that comes out next to the chapel.*

then,' says Gregorio the great-grandson, 'but nowadays our life is not so very different from what it was in the far-off times of the Minorite friars: we sleep more but meditate less.'

'But going down into Toledo can be a time for contemplation,' he adds. 'We can walk from the house along the old lanes that run between garden walls and come out by the bridge of San Martín in a quarter of an hour.' It's a route that recalls memories of when they would walk to the cowshed and milk the cow in the byre.

There was a time when the only way of reaching Madrid was on foot, but now the capital is only half an hour away by high-speed train, which means that Toledo as a poor city of little old ladies in mourning black and skinny Manchegans survives only as a memory. 'Anyway, if Toledo has bowed to modernity,' declares Gregorio, 'it's that type of modernity that has been badly understood and interpreted; what

OPPOSITE AND RIGHT *The original staircase with, around the base of the walls, sixteenth-century glazed tiles. The newel post is topped by a capital carved with Islamic leaf patterns. On the half-landing is a Roman amphora, with another beside the door to the chapel. The antique plasterwork panel above the door came from the Templo de San Juan de la Penitencia.*

could have constituted a fantastic opportunity has resulted in stingy developments of brick-built industrial estates and low-quality commercial conglomerations.'

Leaving the house is to leave behind some of the colour and warmth that comes from the affection that emanates from this *cigarral* - whether its name come from *cigarro* or *cigarra* or whatever.

OPPOSITE *This room was one of the first remodelled by Don Gregorio Marañón. Once the kitchen, it was transformed into a living room, but retains the original fittings, and cooking pans still hang around the fire. The typical round* mesa camilla *is still in use in most rural houses: its tablecloth conceals a holder for hot coals to keep your feet warm while sitting at the table.*

BELOW *The Talavera pottery usually used in the dining room is kept in this built-in cupboard with tile-edged shelves in the adjoining room.*

ABOVE *A painting of St Julian, the cigarral's patron saint, presides over the dining room, formerly the monks' refectory. The table, chairs and bench are all Spanish, while the two lamps hanging over them are fashioned from ecclesiastical censers. The tile wall-panel depicts the Spanish royal coat of arms.*

OPPOSITE *Don Gregorio's library has been kept exactly as he left it. Here he wrote most of his books and would shut himself up to read during his long stays in Toledo, a city he loved.*

RIGHT *Shelves of Spanish classics, including volumes of* Episodios Nacionales *by Benito Pérez Galdós. Don Gregorio was friends with most of the literary and artistic group known as Generación del 98, but he considered Pérez Galdós his mentor.*

OPPOSITE *On one side is a painting of St Julian, to whom the chapel is dedicated, with a painting of the Madonna and several small carvings. The whole chapel is embellished with fragments of Mudéjar cuerda seca tiles that were found in the grounds of the house.*

BELOW *In one corner of the chapel is a collection of religious statues and images, along with reliquaries, processional crosses and other sacred ornaments.*

ABOVE *The chapel is built over an ossuary. Above the main altar is a sixteenth-century Arab plasterwork panel that, unusually for an Islamic work of art, includes representations of human figures.*

OPPOSITE *Olive trees, lavender and cypresses with glimpses of Toledo in the distance. In the foreground can be glimpsed the shrine of St Jerome, which used to belong to the cigarral. The garden was restored in the eighties by the landscaper Maria Medina, who gave it back its original Hispano-Moorish character.*

ABOVE *The veranda, which gives access to the house, with elm trees and a view of Toledo beyond. The cigarral is an example of taking advantage of architectural features that were to hand at the time the house was acquired by Dr Marañón, who salvaged them and sometimes gave them new roles.*

ABOVE *A giant capital from a column has been set upside down to use as a table. The irregular slabs of granite used to build the terrace make it glint in the sunshine. Beyond is a pomegranate grove and, on the left, quince trees.*

Finca Casa de Vacas

MALPICA DE TAJO, CASTILLA-LA MANCHA

The *finca de caza*, or hunting lodge, is a particular type of rural Spanish house. This one is not far from Madrid, along a road bordered by cypresses and lavender that near the house passes by a medieval castle that once belonged to the same family, that of Carlos Falcó y Fernández de Córdova, Marqués de Griñón (and de Castelmoncayo). As well as being a Spanish grandee, the Marqués de Griñón is a highly respected wine-grower and olive-oil producer, and his books reflect his dedication to what he produces.

As in the past, the grapes grown here are Sauvignon, Syrah, Petit Verdot and Graciano. More recently, as a result of his viticultural studies in California, Don Carlos Falcó has developed a computerized irrigation system to reduce the stress on the vines as they grow. As a consequence, in 2003 his Dominio de Valdepusa wine was awarded the first *denominación de origen* recognized in the EU for a single-estate wine. The wine is stored in bodegas standing where cows were once kept, which the *finca* gets its name: Casa de Vacas.

Oils have been pressed on the estate since the thirteenth century, and there are, he says, olive trees here that are more than a thousand years old. A notable pressing is an extra-virgin olive oil called Capilla del Fraile. Why 'del Fraile'? 'The house was built in the eighteenth century,' he explains, 'and when I inherited it there was no electricity or water; it was a tumbledown, rambling place, with enormous rooms. We are talking about simple but very solid construction. There was only one bathroom in the house, and the best room was on the ground floor, which was the curate's room. This came about because the then Señora de Malpica, from the Medinaceli branch of the family, had created a foundation which allowed for the curates of the neighbouring village to look after the chapel, and paid an honorarium to the priest to say mass on Sundays and feast days. It seems the curate would arrive by horse the night before and sleep overnight in "his" room after a copious dinner beside the fire.'

For Don Carlos and his wife, Fátima de la Cierva ('who is passionate about the countryside', he says), this was the family home until 2000, while their daughters were young. Little by little, he brought order to the *finca*, as a result of which the house now has twenty bedrooms, each with

its own bathroom, and the renowned 'Curate's Room' is where King Juan Carlos stays when he comes here to shoot.

The house and the chapel date from 1794 - as does the labourers' cottage, which is now the *bodega*. The chapel is home to a family of owls (symbol of wisdom among the ancient Greeks) and the dining room was formerly the stable and the passage to reach it had a cobbled floor so the horses wouldn't slip. Really, Falco admits, it was an oversized eighteenth-century gamekeeper's house - one with greater luxury than normal as it had a chapel and curate, but for over seven centuries cows were kept where the pool is now situated.

Hunting and shooting encompass a variety of different things. Here in the province of Toledo, the shoot started off with partridges and pheasants: 'the shoots were famous for the quantity of birds and for providing non-stop targets for the guns,' says Falcó. According to Spanish custom, a small-game shooting party has two stages. The first begins at eight in the morning after a breakfast of *churros* with coffee and a shot of *anis*, and the second is divided into four stands, with the two stages broken for an hour for a snack known as the *taco*.

Timings would be different for larger game, but in any case the day would end at six in the evening with a hearty meal, generally a filling stew of chickpeas or butter beans with *chorizo* or ham, or maybe also *gachas*, a very Manchegan porridge-like dish not unlike polenta. At the feast there would surely be no lack of the estate's own wine and the meal would certainly be served on dishes from Puente del Arzobispo. This nearby town has been wholly given over to the manufacture of pottery for more than five hundred years, and they keep the original moulds for a dinner service, which can be personalized with customers' initials or coats of arms.

PREVIOUS PAGE *One of the greatest* fincas *in the environs of Madrid. In the time of the previous* marquess, *its land extended to 10,000ha (25,000 acres) and is known today as the home of one of Spain's most noted wineries: Dominios de Valdepusa.*
ABOVE *An antique Talavera ceramic panel.*
OPPOSITE *The gateway between a* patio *that links the house with the* bodega *and a small botanical garden. The path running through the garden is bordered by cypresses interspersed with olive oil* tinajas, *large urns used for storage.*

OPPOSITE   *The risers of the staircase are decorated with Talavera tiles, and the stone and cobbled floor is the original. The framed photos on the right show the owner's grandfather, dressed for hunting. At one time the house was the estate manager's house, which meant it was austere with no concessions to luxury. Carlos Falcó has retained its very rural character while equipping it all the necessary comforts.*

RIGHT   *The large chest in the entrance hall is Spanish and antique. On it, alongside several bottles of wine, is an ancient book on hunting, while above, either side of the mirror, hang hunting photos and trophies.*

ABOVE *The former kitchen has been converted into an informal dining room, with a medley of china on the shelf above the fireplace and benches and rush-seated chairs around a mesa camilla.*

OPPOSITE *The dining room, once the stables, has exposed beams, simple matting on the floor and plain wooden chairs. Two large built-in wood storage cupboards and vaulted niches house collections of ceramics. The pine table is laid for a hunting supper, with a dinner service from Puente del Arzobispo.*

Monasterio de Lupiana

GUADALAJARA, CASTILLA-LA MANCHA

To reach the Monasterio de Lupiana means crossing the empty plains of Guadalajara province and threading a route through the sun-baked olive-covered hills of La Alcarría. First, there is a glimpse of an ancient ivy-clad wall on the crest of the hill and then, past murmuring streams and dense woodland, there comes into full view the monastery where, in the fourteenth century, the Order of St Jerome was founded in Spain.

According to the official information on the Casa de Lupiana, it began as a primitive chapel, around which grew up a ring of cells 'where a number of hermits dedicated themselves to meditation and sacrifice'. The community of San Bartolomé, as it was known, grew and in 1373 was confirmed as an order by Pope Gregory XI, who himself gave them their habit: 'all wool, the outer tunic white and closed down to the feet, the scapular grey-brown, a small hood and cloak the same'. The order took its name from St Jerome, who was responsible for the Vulgate Bible, the first translation of the Bible from Hebrew to Latin. From this time on the commune's founder was known as Fray Pedro de Guadalajara.

By the sixteenth century the order had become a favourite of King Felipe II, to the extent that some of its monks were installed in his great architectural monument, La Escorial. At around this time the monastery was refashioned and enlarged - the great gateway, styled after Juan de Herrera's work in El Escorial, was added and the vaults were painted with frescoes. Archive records show that by 1786 there were up to 63 servants for the 58 monks and that the monastery owned a number of negro slaves. The Monasterio de San Bartolomé also had a pharmacy, where local peasants and neighbours would come each day to buy herbal cures.

The main entertainment in which the brothers indulged was music - in addition to philosophy, theology and canon law, they were required to study musical scales and singing for up to seven years. The *bartolos*, as they were popularly known, formed chamber orchestras and gave 'truly delightful interpretations' (so says the Lupiana website) of Handel, Bach, Mozart, Beethoven and countless other foreign composers who were introduced to Spain through the Renaissance portals of the monasteries.

At the beginning of the nineteenth century came the devastation of Europe by Napoleon Bonaparte but, in fact, from the point of view of the monks, this couldn't begin to compare with the effect of what followed less than a generation later, when Queen Isabel's *desamortización* disentailed Spain's religious houses. The monks had to abandon Lupiana, the archives conscientiously record, scattering to the four corners of the country and many of them finding employment in musical companies.

'And so ended the history of Lupiana as a

PREVIOUS PAGE *A view of the monastery's cloisters.*
ABOVE *The church was unique in layout and very long, with frescos on its vaulted ceilings, but at the beginning of the twentieth century it collapsed and in the void it left a very unusual, almost magical garden has been created.*
OPPOSITE *The west face of the church is the first sight that greets visitors to the monastery that once belonged to the monks of St Jerome. The triangular pediment carries the arms of Felipe II and above the imposing doorway is a niche holding a statue of St Bartholomew.*

monastery,' says Doña Sol de la Cuesta as she sits in the garden where she used to spend every summer with her family. The monastery passed into private hands in 1836, and Doña Sol's family are the current owner of the estate, which, unusually, has always been passed down the female line. She remarks that growing up among so much religious history translated into a placid, protected life: 'You see the whole edifice as so important - this Renaissance cloister, that historic tower - and you get the feeling of being personally very small and of no account.

'We were looked after by excellent housekeepers, but we would enjoy walking down to the village to buy bread, and as the only girl in the house I would be given tasks to keep me busy - I've even repainted the staircase more than once,' says Doña Sol.

On autumn afternoons they would put on green capes and walk across the fields, which in those days were sown with wheat, barley, corn, alfalfa... 'Even willow was cultivated then, you have no idea of the amazing people who bought it from us for a local manufacturer,' she added. On returning from the walks they would gather

round the fire for a *tertulia*, talking and exchanging ideas in the Spanish version of a literary *salon*. It seems a gilded life, spiced by political and literary friends of her father such as Manuel Góngora, Eduardo Marquina or Agustín de Foxá.

'Is it inconvenient to live here? It's all a question of what you are used to, because we are always adapting ourselves to the needs of the moment.' By way of illustration, Doña Sol points out that, whereas in her grandparents' time this great pile of a house had only two bathrooms and one had to flit down the corridors with candles or oil lamps, nowadays everyone has their own bathroom and light is provided at the flick of a switch.

The house is a complex of buildings and was declared a National Monument in 1931, which is not surprising when you look at some of its detail. The cloister, the work of the mid-sixteenth-century architect Alonso de Covarrubias, is one of the finest of the Spanish Renaissance. Its lower arcade of half-rounded arches has capitals decorated with angels, animals and carved rosettes with medallions. The balustrades are rich with Gothic detail and the galleries have fine coffered ceilings.

Although some of the costs fall entirely on the family, the building is, bit by bit, undergoing a painstaking restoration. Despite this, it was impossible to save the church, which collapsed during the twentieth century. The site is now converted into a romantic garden where one can enjoy the open air among ponds and little fountains that gush water in a scene reminiscent of the Villa Borghese.

The route back to Madrid passes alongside the river Matayeguas and other such scenic spots that can be seen from the house. As one of the comments in the visitors' book says: 'We don't know whether the Brothers of St Jerome were a silent house, but they must have been struck dumb contemplating such a panorama.'

ABOVE *One of the garden's many fountains is the Fount of the Seven Spouts – drink from the central one, it is said, and you will marry.*

OPPOSITE *Part of the garden and the façade that was restored in the 1940s. Felipe II came here on several occasions and among the great architectural accomplishments he would have known, there survive the cloister and the chapter house.*

OPPOSITE *The monastery's 'tradesman's entrance'.*

ABOVE *One of the jewels of the house is the coffered ceiling at the entrance to the cloisters. It originates from the sixteenth century and the wooden panel frames are finely carved.*

RIGHT *The artists who painted the frescos of the lost church are surely the same as these, dedicated to St Barbara, found in the cloisters' antechamber.*

OPPOSITE *The great cloister at Lupiana is one of the treasures of the Spanish Renaissance. It was designed and overseen by Alonso de Coverrubias in 1535 and is decorated with a profusion of motifs (it believed that Covarrubias himself did some of the work), including grapes, rosettes, ribbons and boxes. While the arches of the lower tier are half-rounded, those of the upper tier have a more complicated outline, and the floors are of clay with limestone from a nearby quarry.*

ABOVE *A close-up of the lower arcade of the cloister, showing the arms of the monastic order, and the decorative pierced stonework of the parapet running round the upper tier.*

RIGHT *One of the square-topped 'intercolumnar insertions' by which the architect ingeniously maintained the exact proportions of the cloister. As it has no balustrade, it also provides access to the courtyard. Above it is a classic sundial, which never goes wrong.*

BELOW *In another corner of the study are more photos and a portrait of the previous owner in a ballgown. Even in the middle of the last century, life here was a peaceful one, with friends visiting for leisurely artistic gatherings.*

ABOVE *In the study is a portrait of the owner by the artist Julio Moisés, and on the desk, along with a writing set, are family photos. Reflected in the mirror on the door is the main staircase.*

OPPOSITE *The drawing room, and the dining room beyond, are part of a succession of connecting rooms. Above the doorways are dramatic half-suns in gilded wood. The furniture and paintings are family pieces and it is by this fireplace that they would enjoy lengthy tertulias after an afternoon walk.*

ABOVE *A gallery of the old cloister, called Mudéjar after the Hispano-Moorish style; the monks walled up the arcades in the fifteenth century and the coffered ceiling is in very poor condition. The door leads out into the courtyard with a well that provided the monastery's water.*

OPPOSITE *The floor in the dining room is the original chequered design of slate and limestone. With some builder-friends, Doña Sol's father restored the ceiling himself, dismantling, numbering and reassembling it, along with the ceilings of the drawing room, study and library.*

ABOVE   *Three views of the gardens. The central picture shows 'Grandfather's Garden', romantic in design and studded with statues. In former times the monks put much time and energy into cultivating their herb gardens, and were renowned throughout the region for the medicines made by their apothecaries.*

OPPOSITE   *This doorway, flanked by stone columns, leads from the garden to the cloisters via an antechamber with a coffered ceiling and frescoes. On the garden side of the doors is a stone table at which one can sit, eat and contemplate the impressive view of the river and the valley.*

El Molino de Doña Esperanza

GUADALAJARA, CASTILLA-LA MANCHA

An hour and a half from Madrid, in the province of Guadalajara, is the fertile valley of the River Badiel, a tributary of the Henares, which in turn is a tributary of the Tagus. The floodplain is full of orchards and dotted with thickets among which stands out a house surrounded by elm trees. What can be seen between the trees is a familiar-looking whitewashed construction, and beside the burbling river is an open area of flat ground on which people of various ages are playing *bolos*. This and other clues indicate that this house was once a watermill.

The house, which is at least 350 years old, was at one time called Molino de los Frailes - the friars' mill - as it was home to a community of Benedictines, and as such is mentioned by the brilliant nineteenth-century novelist Benito Pérez Galdós in his *Episodios Nacionales*. Like all watermills, it sits beside a mill pond, which in this instance is 5m (16ft) deep and fed by a channel, the *caz*, that runs water off from the Badiel. Water in the race under the mill would provide enough pressure to drive a turbine whose rotational movement would transmit to the millstones and grind the grain to flour, while the surplus water returned to the river via another channel, the *socaz*.

In years gone by the importance of watermills was considerable in this part of the province, because there was no other way of finding a market for the harvested grain or olives, so the locals brought them to be milled, leaving as payment for the miller a share of the milling called the *maquila*.

El Molino de Esperanza is basic in its construction, with stone and mud walls at least 60cm (2ft) thick. The structural woodwork is of elm and pine, following the old saying: *el olmo, pino, y el pino tumbado* - elm stands up and pine falls down - so the uprights are of elm and the crossbeams are pine. Both storeys of the mill are now used as living space. The ground floor comprises a living room, which was the old milling hall, a dining room, which used to be the stables, a kitchen, a bedroom and a bathroom. On the upper floor, which is where the miller slept, there is another bathroom and three more bedrooms. Decoration is simple and well-chosen to set off some antique pieces, apart from which paintings by the current owners decorate the walls and vases overflow with wild meadow flowers.

'Whoever lives here not only has to maintain the structure of the mill, but has to keep it running, so that you can enjoy the musicality of the water right inside yourself.' This is the Madrid architect Alberto Martín-Artajo speaking. He is the owner with his wife Esperanza, who has not only given the mill her name but also her spirit, as well as much of its artistic and domestic ambience.

Ties to the area have led this respected architect to expand his already busy workload by setting up a family business renovating old mills and former industrial buildings such as electrical sub-stations, with the aim of turning them into homes with a different sort of charm from the typical holiday chalet. He finds there is a growing interest in a lifestyle that isn't city-based.

Together with their children and grandchildren, Alberto and Esperanza keep a small poultry flock, as well as a seasonal fruit and vegetable garden that provides enough for family consumption. The fertiliser they use to enrich the plot is largely poultry manure mixed with humus made from composted elm leaves.

Relations with their neighbours are usually excellent, they say, being based on a mutual respect, with profound opinions and, above all, valuable knowledge often being exchanged in casual discussions. 'The life that we have here at El Molino can't be divorced from its environment, and so, shopping in the nearby towns... constitutes a little event that always breaks the monotony.'

PREVIOUS PAGE *The old mill pond has been converted into a swimming pool, its icy waters ringed by plum trees, black poplars and vegetation.*
ABOVE *The front door is solid wood and ironwork, including antique hand-forged nails and door-knocker.*
OPPOSITE *The dining room is on the ground floor, next to the sitting room but at a lower level, and adjoins the kitchen. There is an extendable table and antique chairs, and from the ceiling hang paper lampshades, while on the window sill sit glass jars of home-made conserves.*

OPPOSITE *The living room is in the old milling hall. One of its most notable occupants today is a statue of St Antonio Bendito, the local patron saint. The fire surround has a border of antique glazed tiles. Above it hangs an ironic photo of the owners dressed in the traditional local dress and to its right is a portrait of the architect by Segura. In the foreground is a* mesa camilla *covered in a red damask cloth.*

RIGHT *In the sitting area of the living room more of the mill's original beams have been retained. The sofa bases have been constructed from brick faced with plaster and wood.*

LEFT *The main bedroom is upstairs, where the original wood beams are exposed, outlining the shape of the roof. The bedspreads on the antique beds are from Provence.*

ABOVE *All the ingenuity that went into the old mills has been preserved here. This is a view towards the entrance to the house, beside the channel that diverts the river water from the mill pond.*

OPPOSITE *Just outside the main door is a favourite place for the family to gather at the end of the day, when conversation is accompanied by the constant gentle burble of water through the old channels.*

Alquería del Pí

ALBORAYA, VALENCIA

Once it would take nearly two hours by horse and carriage to get here from Valencia, but nowadays (depending on the traffic), it can be just a mere few minutes' drive through the fertile fields of the Huerta. The Alquería del Pí, also known as Alquería de San José, is built on the foundations of a Moorish house that later belonged to the Church until it was confiscated in the nineteenth-century *desamortización*; since then it has belonged to just one family. It is 15km (10 miles) from the centre of Valencia and just 2km (a mile or so) inland from the beach at Alboraya, the focus of a small rural community grouped around the chapel of San José. At first sight the main building has a half-colonial, half-Italian appearance, and in spring the heady scent from the surrounding sea of orange blossom can knock you senseless.

The region of the Levante in general and around Valencia in particular is rich agricultural land: the very name Huerta means orchard or kitchen garden. As well as oranges, olives and vines, there are mulberry trees here, food for the silkworms that for hundreds of years were vital to the local textile industry. This was the land of the Phoenicians and the Romans, the Moors and the Christians, but first and foremost it belongs to the Mediterranean. But it is a land with two faces: one happy and shining, raucous and festive; the other darker, governed by a constant fight for water rights and ancestral rulings such as the Solomon-like Tribunal de Las Aguas. This darker side, which gives Valencianos a reserved, at times even hostile air, was what the writer Blasco Ibañez so sharply observed in his novels in which he described the customs and passions of life in the *alquerías* and *barracas* around Valencia.

No one is very clear about the roots of the word *alquería*, which seems to come from the Arab *carya*, meaning labourer's house or a settlement that is neither town nor fortified stronghold. But such a vague definition could apply to almost any Spanish rural house. What is certain, says Francisco Pérez de los Cobos in his book *Alquerías, masías y heredades de Valencia*, is that an *alquería* is the type of house found in the belt of countryside between the mountains and the coast and with land devoted to major crops: groves of orange and orange blossom, rows of almond trees, vines and, always, always, the inevitable olive. It is, in short, associated with large-scale agriculture,

whereas if it were a smallholding, it would be a *barraca*.

Despite the *alqueria's*, etymologically speaking, Moorish origins, its roots are in the Roman villa, which proliferated throughout the agriculturally prosperous Spanish Levante during Roman rule. But *alquerias* also multiplied under the Moors when, to a certain extent, they were associated with defence as well as farming.

Alquerias are distinguished by their smooth, plastered walls and their rectangular outline, like *masias*; almost all have two storeys topped a large loft and a turret or belvedere. The main façade always faces east, with a round-arched entrance and a veranda-like *porche* where much of life is carried on, with a terrace above that keeps the house cool in summer. The west-

ABOVE *A detail of the dining room's painted ceiling, with its triangular cross-beams.*
OPPOSITE *The first-floor dining room is an unusual room. Its walls are completely decorated with frescos by Francesc Pla, depicting coastal, rural and urban scenes, with a curtain-like border painted all around the top. Through the doorway can be seen the study, with an English writing desk and a family portrait.*

facing façade, sheltered from the east wind, usually includes a place to sit and enjoy the view on winter afternoons.

On the ground floor is the *llar*, with its fireplace under a great chimney hood, for cooking, and the *estudi* or master bedroom. Traditionally this would be where the clothes chests were kept, along with a shotgun for defence, the family treasures and the more vulnerable and costly agricultural tools. A typical piece of furniture would be a very high bed of carved or painted wood: the *camó* or matrimonial bed.

A staircase in one corner would lead up to the other bedrooms and then up again to the *andana*. This spacious loft area would be used for storing the harvest and also for raising silkworms, for Valencia was once famous for its silks and brocades.

The Alquería del Pi, surrounded by its extensive fields, was built in 1836 and has features, notably its turret, that give it a Florentine look. Although every *alqueria* has such a little tower, from which to see the sea in the distance, this one rises up from the centre of the roof and clearly has a Lombard influence in the shape of its eaves and

crenellations. It is one of the details that define it as a house of leisure rather than of labour, although it has a full range of service areas, where the caretakers now live, that includes stables and stableyard, courtyards, granaries, a well, a dovecote and the *andana*.

When Don José Maria Giménez Fayos, an important figure in the cultural and intellectual life of Valencia in the twentieth century, inherited the house it became renowned for its *tertulias* or artistic gatherings. On summer evenings visitors such as the Marqués de Lozoya or the painters Salvador Tuset and Federico Badenes, who both painted views of the house, would arrive from Valencia in carriages and stroll around the romantic garden, refreshing themselves with lemonade or *horchata*, Valencia's cooling almond drink.

Don José's daughter, Doña Maria Amparo Giménez Borja, and later his grandchildren, have put real passion and effort into conserving this *alqueria*. Doña Maria is responsible, among other things, for the restoration of the frescos from the school of Francesc Pla that decorate the walls and ceiling of a *salón* on the main floor. Her father collected anything that claimed his attention, from dolls' houses to Neapolitan figurines, and in his day the house held a fine collection of ceramics, including eighteenth-century decorative tile panels from nearby Alcora or Manises. He also had a collection of cameras and was a gifted amateur photographer with - a rarity - his own darkroom. The images of the Huerta and rural scenes that he captured and that his descendants have inherited are an important testimony to rural life here in times gone by.

ABOVE *The stairwell is used to display an important collection of antique ceramic panels.*

OPPOSITE *The double doors in the main hallway used to be where the carriages would come and go, and the wheel ruts can still be seen on the floor. The dado tiling is a Sevillan type known as 'diamond point', and the two ceramic panels hanging above the monastic chair are eighteenth century from Manises and typically Valencian. As in many houses in the Huerta, the kitchen is behind a curtained doorway.*

OPPOSITE *In the Huerta the kitchen is known as the llar, and this one has the typical big fireplace that would be used for cooking and be the focus of everyday life, a large sink and a well. An indoor well, always covered, was very common, as it avoided the need to go outside for water in cold or rainy weather.*

BELOW *The stone sink in which clothing would be washed. The wall tiles are local, from Manises, and the various china and ceramic pieces beside the sink include some shaving bowls.*

ABOVE *The piano room, nowadays a sitting room, would originally have been the estudi or master bedroom. The chequered floor is made of earthenware tiles and Manises ceramic tiles.*

OPPOSITE *The Casita de Piedra – stone cottage – is what successive generations of owners have called 'the little building at the end of the garden', which serves no other purpose than to provide somewhere to take the air and contemplate the view. As well as the arched entrance there are openings to either side and another in the roof to allow the breeze to flow through.*

ABOVE *A view of the house from the casita. This is the west-facing side, favoured in winter, and the belvedere in the turret is an ideal place to enjoy the winter sun.*

RIGHT *A detail from the casita's ceiling. The inside walls are entirely covered in frescos.*

Moncaire

MALLORCA, ISLAS BALEARES

Due to its geographical location, the island of Mallorca has suffered constant invasions, and Romans, Byzantines, Moors and Catalans have all contributed to a rich cultural legacy. Following his conquest in 1229, King Jaime of Aragon and Cataluña parcelled out land among his nobles, who were wealthy landowners on the mainland, but especially among his knights, who became landowners for the first time. This became known historically as the *rempartment*, and had a deep influence of the territorial divisions of the island that can still be seen today.

From the seventeenth, but especially in the eighteenth century, Italian influences travelled across the Mediterranean and Mallorcan architecture acquired characteristics that began to distinguish it from other parts of Spain. Country houses were converted into true rural palaces, with no skimping on typically Italian ornamental detailing, such as coloured stucco, façades embellished by balconies and loggias with wrought iron railings. The layout would usually include a central courtyard called the *clastra*, from which led off various offices, the storehouses, the granary or the olive oil press.

Moncaire is a very large *finca*, situated high in the Tramontana range than runs parallel to the coast from south-west to north-east. It is hard to reach, like all properties in these mountains, and the isolation of these mountain *fincas* emphasizes their difference from those on the plain below. Mallorcan country houses usually form part of a working estate, but whereas in the mountains they would be geared to the making and storing of olive oil, their lowland counterparts would have capacious storehouses for grain and straw. In the past, as well as providing a home for the landowners, these large houses also served as a defence - against pirate attack near the coast, and from banditry inland. (Since time immemorial, it was customary for the main gateway to be locked at dusk and the keys kept by the steward or head of the household staff, who would live with his family outside the gates.)

Moncaire sits 500m (1600ft) above sea level in a high valley, sheltered by the surrounding peaks and by thousand-year-old olive trees with trunks up to 4m (13ft) in diameter. It faces south-west and the views of the Mediterranean from its terrace are magnificent. The original construction of

the house, which included a lovely chapel, dates from the seventeenth century. Its interior has recently been remodelled to provide six bedrooms with bathrooms, a gym, a TV room and home cinema, a dining room and a red-painted library with an umbrella-pine floor. The living room, with its high, pitched ceiling, once housed the oil press. Beams and woodwork were salvaged, and a few pieces of stone protruding from the walls remain as a reminder of its original role.

The old piggery in the grounds has been converted into an outdoor summer dining room, beside a formal herb garden full of aromatic plants. Close by is the *alberca*, the water reservoir, reached via a delightful path that starts from the tower and winds between lavender and Moncaire's grapevines, which are capable of producing some 500 bottles of Chardonnay. The swimming pool, though, is something else. Its warm waters are fed by a nearby spring and, exotically, it is set among boulders among which one can swim while contemplating the blue sea on one side and the tennis courts on the other.

Although in principle this type of mountain

finca cannot be fully classified a typical Mallorcan *possessió*, *it has* some elements in common because of shared economy and history. The dictionary definition of a *possessió* is 'an expanse of terrain under cultivation, belonging to one owner and with a house on the estate'. In this sense, Moncaire is a *possessió*, but it fits the bill in other ways too. A typical *possessió* has been described as a rural yet noble house, tall and elegant, with a central courtyard or *clastra* and often with a tower for defence.

Stone is an essential element in the Balearic Islands. According to the learned architect Carlos Flores in his classic *La Casa popular española*, it is not possible to talk of a vernacular architecture common to all the islands, but there is a single material that

PREVIOUS PAGE *Moncaire seen across the reservoir, with the Sierra de Tramontana rising up behind.*
ABOVE *Shallow steps bordered by shrubby santolinas lead to the four-storey tower part of the house.*
OPPOSITE *The central courtyard, the* clastra, *is an integral part of every Mallorcan house. The staircase with the wrought iron handrail on the right leads up to the guest bedroom and the library.*

predominates: a limestone known as *marès*, which 'being abundant and easy to obtain throughout the archipelago, constitutes the fundamental element of vernacular construction'. This stone is so soft that it can be cut easily, even with a handsaw, and in Mallorcan buildings it is frequently seen left bare, rather than covered up with plaster or whitewash. It is exactly this stone that has been used for the archway of Moncaire's stubby tower. As was typical for a seventeenth-century manor house, the archway is guarded by a gate made of olive wood with glass insets.

In addition to the main house and a guest cottage, there is a third house, which is home to the gatekeeper and staff, modern-day successors to those servants who, in times gone by, would close the gates at dusk and guard the key until the next morning.

OPPOSITE   *The top room of the tower, directly beneath its roof, has been made into a studio-cum-belvedere, furnished with low day-beds and rugs.*

ABOVE   *The seventeenth-century chapel with its original altarpiece.*

Much of Moncaire's past is typical of most, if not all, country houses of a certain age in Spain, but it's more recent history is rather more unusual. When a Lao Champassac prince (the last husband of Woolworth heiress Barbara Hutton), fled Laos, he decided to settle on the other side of the world, in Spain and, more particularly, on Mallorca. He chose a house lost in the mountains where, despite all the access difficulties, the views of the azure sea and the scents and flavours of the earth's produce must have compensated somewhat for the isolation. That house was Moncaire, and it was here that the eccentric prince founded a Buddhist centre.

In due course, Moncaire came into the possession of its present owners, Diana and Philippe Harari, who, ten years ago, decided to take on its restoration with the Mallorcan architect Antonio Obrador, without whose splendid work it would not be possible today to experience its many delights.

OPPOSITE *The inner hall, with a long-case clock and a hat-stand laden with straw sunhats. The courtyard is through the door on the right. Restoration work has been slow and laborious, salvaging the original* marés *stone, cleaning up all the facilities and reinstating the original layout.*

ABOVE *Through this curtained archway steps lead down to the main entrance hall, with its cobbled floor and antique* tinajas *that once held olive oil and wine.*

LEFT *A floral tapestry from the late seventeenth century. The stone floor is original.*

ABOVE *One end of the living room, with English eighteenth-century chairs around a backgammon table. The oil painting above the sofa is by the Mallorcan painter Menéndez Rojas. The doorway in the far corner leads to the tower's spiral staircase.*

OPPOSITE *The living room, once the room where the oil was pressed, had been a complete wreck. The original beams and roof trusses were saved and the fireplace rebuilt, but the stairs and stair-rail are new, built from olive wood. A few stones embedded in the walls hint at the original structure and use. The painting over the fireplace is of the Virgin of Cuzco.*

ABOVE *The two round tables in the dining room are covered with cloths made from antique Moroccan tenting fabric. The chimney breast has been completely rebuilt and the typically Mallorcan niches on either side house a collection of antique glass.*

OPPOSITE *The library's red walls were created from a mix of pigments. The umbrella-pine floorboards survive from the original house, as do the ceiling beams.*

OPPOSITE *White is the predominant colour in the main bedroom, where the bed has barley-twist posts but no canopy. This room is in the tower, along with the other private rooms of the owners.*

ABOVE *The porche, with the tower on one side and the reservoir, with far views of the sea, on the other. The chairs are very Mallorcan in design, and were made in wrought iron by Denario.*

LEFT *One of the bedrooms under the eaves in the guest cottage.*

ABOVE *The shape of the pool was designed around one large rock in the grounds, to which others were added to make a sort of natural pool, so that one can swim among the rocks with the sea as a backdrop.*

RIGHT *The former piggery has been converted into a summer dining area, looking out over a herb garden planted in a chequerboard design.*

Alcuzcuz

SAN PEDRO DE ALCÁNTARA, ANDALUCIA

On the final stretch of road to Alcuzcuz from Ronda there's a long bend fringed with greenery - you can see snails clinging to the vegetation - and then there comes into view a stand of cork trees with, beyond it, the breathtaking sight of the blue sea touched by the morning's mist.

In between is a large pink house ringed by cypresses reaching up to the sky, and glimpses of a dream of a garden. 'You ask,' says its owner, the interior designer Jaime Parladé, 'whether we should plant non-native species in this parched ground. Of course we shouldn't, but who can resist the temptation to try something new?' Just the sort of response you would expect from someone part-Andalucian, part-Basque who lived in the melting pot of Tangiers in the 1940s, where at one time he had a shop selling wicker furniture. 'My roots in Morocco go deep,' he says. 'It's where I lived for the first twenty years of my life, and that land, and the eccentricity and cosmopolitan sophistication that reigned there during my youth, had a marked effect on me.'

At last, we enter the house, crossing the hallway into an inner *patio*. Here, an enormous oil painting colourfully depicts Jaime's shop, complete with a portrait of himself and all those involved in it. Also in the *patio* is a ceramic panel. It says that Alcuzcuz (which, with a coincidental nod to Jaime's early life, means 'couscous') was built in 1884 by Jaime's grandfather and then partly destroyed by fire in 1917 but that its restoration did not begin until the middle of the twentieth century. Jaime explains that his grandfather, also called Jaime Parladé, was a gentleman who had been brought up among the great olive-farm *cortijos* around Seville, and these were what inspired his restoration of the house, which he did with great taste and aplomb but on a more modest scale appropriate to Málaga province. Alcuzcuz had only one crop, cork, apart from what the goats provided, and it became a country *finca*, although, Jaime adds: 'to call this explosion of housing estates that now surrounds us "countryside" is pretty hypocritical.' The creeping urbanization clearly saddens him.

A century after it was built, and after much renovation (Jaime's parents had lived in the house before passing it on to him), Alcuzcuz finally became home in 1986 to its present owners: Jaime and Janetta, Janetta and Jaime.

'I remember,' he goes on, 'when we were moving into Alcuzcuz, after eighteen years at the Torre de Tramores. In mid-move, the house full of boxes, furniture standing around forlornly, nothing in its place and everything looking its worst, Janetta went out into the garden, which was also then pretty pathetic, brought in a leafy branch and laid it on the fireplace. Suddenly, everything felt warm and alive.'

It is his golden-haired English wife, a friend in their day of Gerald Brenan, Virginia Woolf and all the flourishing Bloomsbury Group, that Jaime toasts with this accolade. Her touch is special, he says, because the house is always filled with flowers, the fires always lit. 'Even when we go to our apartment in Madrid, Janetta will usually first go out into the garden here to pick a bunch of flowers which, carefully wrapped in damp newspaper and plastic, just need arranging when we arrive at the flat. The English are the queens of comfort,' he asserts.

'When we were moving here in the eighties she said the house needed a change of colour. The result, which appears rosy from a distance, is not so much pink as red ochre. Jaime painted it this colour despite it always having been whitewashed, simply because he remembered old photos in which he could discern colour on the walls between the climbers. Nobody else remembered this, but the restoration work confirmed it: underneath many layers of whitewash there came to light just that type of strong pink - so that's how its colour came to be restored.

Janetta certainly brings colour Jaime's life, and anyone who has met her for even five minutes will know that, winter or summer, life

PREVIOUS PAGE: *The house was built in the nineteenth century by Jaime Parladé's great-grandmother, the Condesa de Aguiar and takes its name from a nearby hill near San Pedro de Alcántara.* ABOVE: *Among the pictures on the hallway wall is a tile painting by Jean Cocteau, dedicated to the house's owners.*

OPPOSITE *The cobbled hallway at Alcuzcuz is made, as is traditional locally, from beach pebbles, and built-in benches provide somewhere for waiting callers to sit. Beyond the Andalucian wrought iron grille is the patio, in the centre of which is a fountain in Sierra Elviera stone, which came from a house in Granada's Moorish quarter, the Albaicín.*

within the walls of Alcuzcuz is a rich one. Mealtimes are inclined to be irregular and they'll eat in different parts of the house, according to the weather. 'Living here is pure glory,' says Jaime. 'The old gatehouse, down the end of the track that leads up to the house, is my studio and there's a tumbledown shop that's like my Aladdin's Cave, full of things to incorporate into my work.' For Janetta, devoting herself for hours to painting and the garden, Alcuzcuz is a bastion of tranquillity. 'Nevertheless,' adds Jaime Parladé, 'for me, although I enjoy Alcuzcuz enormously, I don't think a bastion of tranquillity is my ideal habitat.'

Once inside Alcuzcuz one certainly feels inside a retreat, or rather a series of retreats - living rooms, dining room and kitchen, with terraces leading off them giving views over the garden to the sea - where the dominant factor is an ordered hotch-potch of Spanish and English ceramics, rare books and even rarer textiles. It almost resembles a stage set, with elements from every imaginable style, from Baroque to Classical via Modernista. And then you go out into the garden...

Here the colourful exuberance of primulas, plumbagos as well as exotic shrubs such as philodendrons, frangipane and who knows what else, is a floral delight at every turn - around the pool as well as by the little shrine and in the conservatory, with plantings cleverly punctuated by stone busts and other statuary.

Jaime once said in an interview that the furnishing of the house was down to him but, as his wife has such exquisite taste, whenever he had any doubts he turned to her and she came up with the perfect solution. Janetta and Jaime seem to have, what a traditional Spanish saying would have called, a marriage of hunger with a joy of eating.

ABOVE *Through this doorway can be seen a pine console table holding antique ceramics and a scene of Alcuzcuz. The mirror above is from Provence.*
OPPOSITE *Near the house entrance these two painted alcoves, equipped with rails and shelves, act as coat cupboards. Between them, on a pedestal, is an eighteenth-century carved bust of a Roman emperor. Behind the bust is a small tiled altarpiece dedicated to St James the Apostle.*

OPPOSITE *Dominating a wall of the sitting room is a painted wall-cloth that came from a palace in Cádiz province. Other paintings in the room come from Jaime's grandfather's house, of which his favourite is a portrait of Isabel de Valois. The rugs are Indian dhurries, and the table is one of Parladé's own designs, made from an old door and finials from curtain rails.*

BELOW *Jaime Parladé and his wife Janetta both like to cook and eat with friends in this dining area which is extension of the kitchen. The sideboard holds a collection of china dinner services and the rustic tables are Portuguese. On the walls are displayed ceramics from Granada and paintings by various artists, many of them their friends.*

LEFT *The library is next to the sitting room and leads directly out in to the garden. The painting above the antique marble fireplace is a nude by James Guthrie, one of the Glasgow Boys. To either side of the fireplace is a games table and in front a leather-padded fender seat.*

BELOW *An eighteenth-century carving of a horse stands on a marble table, with fresh-picked flowers from the garden.*

ABOVE *In another corner of the library hangs an eighteenth-century still-life with, below it, two bull-fighting scenes that may be by Chaves. Among the miscellaneous items on the shelf are a terracotta figurine of the designer's great-grandmother and a collection of polished stone eggs.*

LEFT *The interior of the chapel, painted a rich red ochre. The chapel was originally inside the house but it was moved out of the grounds into a clearing in the cork trees, reached along a path beside the swimming pool that joins a lane running between Benahavis and San Pedro de Alcántara. The chapel's original location was turned into a guest room decorated with a Moorish theme.*

OPPOSITE *The chapel's Baroque altarpiece, bought by Parladé's grandfather when he built the chapel, depicts St Joseph, to whom the chapel is dedicated and who is a favourite saint within local area – the chapel is the focus of a romería or local pilgrimage, for the neighbouring villages.*

ABOVE *Janetta redesigned the garden to give it a very Andalucian style, with sandy paths, decorative iron grilles, secluded areas providing outdoor 'rooms' and many aromatic plants, combining to create a certain air of mystery and magic.*

OPPOSITE *The patio provides a large, sheltered area to relax, enlivened by an amusing painting by Nicoletta Sinclair in which Parladé and his team are portrayed.*

OPPOSITE *An enormous jacaranda welcomes visitors as they arrive at the house.*

BELOW *A garden path runs under tunnels of hibiscus, morning glories, wisteria and jacarandas – a symphony of blues and mauves whose fallen petals cover the sandy path like a carpet.*

ABOVE *The swimming pool is situated beside a terrace largely unseen from the house. Lined in white and surrounded by terracotta tiles it is sheltered by aromatic hedges and large flower pots.*

Cortijo El Patronato

ANDALUCIA

Catalina was an illegitimate daughter of the Conde de Bailén who, having been a slave-girl in a nobleman's house, was given her freedom in sixteen hundred and something. The story goes that, on becoming a free woman, she rode across Castille on horseback to reach and take charge of the lands she had inherited from her father.

In due course, Doña Catalina decreed in her will that the convent of Santa Clara in the nearby town of Estepa should be the beneficiary of her goods and income, adding them to the existing *patronato* or foundation under their auspices; which is how the house got its name.

Now, as then, the white farmhouse nestles into the surrounding landscape, encircled by low hills over which partridges fly and rabbits graze. The cultivated areas of the estate are both extensive and varied, but even in 1677, according to the nuns' records, there was 'a gate house and bullpen and straw loft, plus 44 *fanegas* [nearly 30 ha or 70 acres] of tilled land with 37 of vines and 610 of olive trees'.

Two centuries later the nuns lost their land and their property in Isabel II's *desamortización*, and El Patronato has since remained in private hands. But whoever owned the land, right up to the present day, has never given up cultivating olives.

As almost everywhere in Andalucía, the art of olive-growing here is accorded a status that is more than just an art, it's an inherent part of the culture. Its end product - olive oil - is now recognized by everyone as an asset to a healthy diet (one TV commercial referred to it, while showing a beating human heart, as 'the best oil for your engine'). Beside the gateway to El Patronato is a ceramic tile panel that reads, in Latin: *Olea Prima Omnium Arborum Est* - a quote from the first-century Roman agronomist Lucio Columela which translates as: The olive is the first among all the trees.

El Patronato sits in the geographical heart of Andalucía and is typical of *cortijos* of old. It still has a central courtyard or *patio* surrounded by grain stores and a stable full of horses and donkeys, and an old mill houses ancient presses and dozens of hundred-year-old *tinajas*, the enormous pot-bellied earthenware jars used to store thousands of litre of olive oil each season. And presiding over

it all is the bell-gable of the little chapel.

Apart from the telephone and electricity, the *cortijo*'s interior has changed little since the time of the poor Clares. A row of bedrooms recall the nuns' cells, and the chapel's bell rings out at lunchtime in summer so that those who are bathing in the reservoirs know that in 20 minutes they should be seated at the dining table. These reservoirs, or tanks, formed part of the irrigation system of the old kitchen garden, and nowadays are a favourite with the family during the torrid summer months – this is a region where the very dryness and heat bring out the scenery's greatest beauty but where, for example, water jugs need to be kept filled, because the tapwater is undrinkable.

In winter, on the other hand, it's a pleasure to retire after a meal to drink coffee beside the

Opposite   The ancient well and water trough to which the horses and mules would be brought to drink every day. In the background is the main gateway to the cortijo *and, on the right, a cross on a Roman column that has been regularly whitewashed for centuries.*

ABOVE *Round roosting perches in the dovecote.*

fire in the upstairs *salón* and look out over a vista that stretches to the Sierra Nevada. The view is much the same now as when the gentry of El Patronato would put on their hats and set off in their traps or open carriages to pay a visit to neighbouring *cortijos*.

The family that lives here now had always understood that El Patronato dated back to the seventeenth century, but one day chance arrived to stretch that history right back to the fourth century AD, with a discovery that was documented at the time to be of major importance to the history of Roman Spain.

One morning about twenty years ago Doña María Jesús Martín-Artajo got up and said to her grandchildren: 'Come on, children, put your hats on and get on the tractor; we're going treasure-hunting.' Bumping along the tracks of the *finca*, Doña María Jesús explained: 'When you see a mound that is whiter than others around it, it could be because its soil contains remains of construction materials.'

Arriving at a promising hillock, each of them began to scratch away at the surface, hunting for ceramic shards, and barely five minutes had passed before Doña María came

across a solid, cold, and compacted surface, like a floor. She began to clear the loose soil while calling the children, who came rushing to her side. Only when the hole was big enough could they make out something. 'The Virgin, Grandma! It's the Virgin Mary!' cried one little girl after putting her head in the hole, and soon they could all see at the bottom of their excavation a face encircled by what looked like a saintly halo.

Doña María sent for more help from the *cortijo*, and half an hour later the rest of the household arrived, led by her husband, Joaquín Fernández de Santaella. They all stared amazed at the ground where, between the clods of earth, there had appeared an image of a group of five figures delicately picked out in innumberable multi-coloured tesserae, shining like glazed pottery (see illustration on page 6) .

It didn't take long to realize that what they were seeing was the Judgement of Paris. Grandfather Joaquín chucked a bucket of water over the mosaic and Aphrodite, the Greek goddess of love, gleamed out from the soil. She was dressed in a cape that was completely transparent in front, and wearing garters from which hung ankle-length fringes. Aphrodite, her companions, and Paris were all contained within a border of golden wheat ears in just the same magnificent state of conservation.

Bending over so the little ones could hear him better, Grandfather Joaquín explained that Betica - the Romans' name for Andalucía - was the granary of the Empire, and so it was here that the Roman patricians built the finest villas on the most flourishing cereal farms.

The next day the archeologists arrived and uncovered the foundations of the villa, a funerary urn, Honorio coins, not to mention a total of 25 mosaics, including the Judgement of Paris, which can today be admired in Seville's Museo Arqueológico.

ABOVE *A sandy corner of the garden, with an oleander in bloom.*
OPPOSITE *The windows of the bedrooms that were formerly the nuns' cells look out over the kitchen garden. They still have their old grilles and the Cordoban mats in the foreground provide shade from the heat of the sun. The wall buttresses are the sort known in Andalucía as* pie de amigo, *or friend's foot.*

OPPOSITE *The dining room on the ground floor. The table is covered by an antique cashmere shawl and on the sideboard a tea set and various pieces of silver. On the mantelpiece are displayed seventeenth-century Talavera ceramics, including a barber's bowl.*

BELOW *In a corner of the* salón *stands an old Basque longcase clock signed Abásolo, a mahogany armchair and a Baroque carved niche with a saint holding a silver-handled riding whip.*

ABOVE *A view of the upstairs* salón, *which opens on to the terrace overlooking the main kitchen garden. A bronze lamp hangs in the foreground, and also notable are a hazelwood chair and the desk from the era of Felipe II.*

OPPOSITE *The mares and donkeys at their mangers – with little Juana in the foreground – in stables roofed with olive-wood beams.*

BELOW *Harnesses no longer in use, but including yokes for the mule teams that well into the last century were absolutely vital to rural work.*

ABOVE *An open cooking fire, where until the middle of the twentieth century the farm's labourers would cook their lunch. The floor is cobbled and horseshoes adorn the chimney breast.*

THESE PAGES: *The tiny chapel in the middle of the cortijo's cobbled patio. What looks like a spiral column (to the left of the entrance) is, in fact, a screw from the old olive press. The bronze bell, green with age, carries an inscription that reads* Ora Pro Nobis Santa Clara *(Pray for us, St Clare). Inside the chapel is a gilded image of the Virgin Mary.*

ACKNOWLEDGEMENTS

ANDALUCÍA
Sres. de Fernández de Santaella, Don Joaquín
Sres. de Parladé, Don Jaime
Doña Maria Pilar Aritio

VALENCIA
Don Francisco Pérez de los Cobos
Don Antonio y don Borja Monzó

CATALUÑA
Doña Carmen Guell
Don Mariano Sanz-Briz Klein
Don Carlos Aguilera, Conde de Fuenrubia

EXTREMADURA
Don Duarte Pinto Coelho

CASTILLA LA MANCHA
Sres. de Martín Artajo, Don Alberto
Doña Sol de la Cuesta
Don Gregorio Marañón Beltrán de Lys
Don Alejandro Fernández Araoz
Don Carlos Falcó, Marqués de Griñón

CASTILLA LEON
Don Francisco y Doña Sabine Muñoz

PAIS VASCO
Don Iñigo de Begoña
Don Beltrán Hormaechea
Doña Pilar Orbe
Doña Tona Prado

GALICIA
Señor de Rubianes
Don Alfonso Muñoz

ISLAS BALEARES
Philip and Diana Harari